Basil - charity
          trade
Ambrose - common ownership
          usufruct
p104 Causes of scarcity
106 Charity Solution
107 Cryostism → Communism

THE ECONOMIC PROBLEM
IN
BIBLICAL AND PATRISTIC THOUGHT

SUPPLEMENTS TO

VIGILIAE CHRISTIANAE

Formerly Philosophia Patrum

TEXTS AND STUDIES OF EARLY CHRISTIAN LIFE
AND LANGUAGE
EDITORS

J. DEN BOEFT — A. F. J. KLIJN — G. QUISPEL
J. H. WASZINK — J. C. M. VAN WINDEN

VOLUME IX

THE ECONOMIC PROBLEM
IN
BIBLICAL AND PATRISTIC THOUGHT

BY

BARRY GORDON

University of Newcastle, New South Wales

E.J. BRILL

LEIDEN · NEW YORK · KØBENHAVN · KÖLN
1989

By the same author

Non-Ricardian Political Economy
Economic Analysis Before Adam Smith: Hesiod to Lessius
Political Economy in Parliament, 1819-1823
Economic Doctrine and Tory Liberalism, 1824-1830

HB
72
.G67
1988

Library of Congress Cataloging-in-Publication Data

Gordon, Barry J.
  The economic problem in biblical and patristic thought / by Barry
Gordon.
    p.   cm.—(Supplements to Vigiliae Christianae, ISSN
0042-6032; v. 9)
  Bibliography: p.
  Includes index.
  ISBN 90-04-09048-7
  1. Economics—Moral and ethical aspects—History. 2. Economics—
Religious aspects—Christianity—History. I. Title. II. Series.
HB72.G67   1988
174'4—dc19   89-754
                                                         CIP

ISSN   0042-6032
ISBN   90 04 09048 7

PRINTED IN THE NETHERLANDS BY E. J. BRILL

For
*Allan, Justin, Mark,
Hugh, and Ian,*
my sons.

CONTENTS

PREFACE

For most modern economists, the economic problem is the problem of scarcity. Most appear to be in broad, general agreement with the understanding of the foundations of Economics as depicted by Lionel Robbins in his influential, *An Essay on the Nature and Significance of Economic Science* (1932). Yet, few of these economists reflect on the fact that scarcity has been a continuing element of the human condition, and that, as a consequence, serious regard for the issue is present in much of the literature which long pre-dates even the beginnings of the emergence of Economics as a discipline. This book is about some of that early literature, and it involves a survey of thought extending from 800 B.C. to A.D. 400.

The book begins with a study of the treatment of scarcity by the Yahwist, one of the first contributors to the Old Testament. The Yahwist explored the nature and origins of scarcity, and he put forward two, general strategies for dealing with the problem. These were, the Solution by Faith and, the Solution by Wisdom (Chapter One). In subsequent Jewish thought, the latter were replaced by the Solution by Observance of the Law (Chapter Two). Over the centuries between the destruction of the first Temple in Jerusalem (587 B.C.) and its partial restoration by the Maccabeans (164 B.C.) there were further initiatives. One of these was the Solution by Mediation (Chapter Three). Another was the Apocalyptic Solution (Chapter Four).

With the New Testament, there is a radical change of perspective (Chapter Five). In the Sermon on the Mount, Jesus proposes his Solution by Seeking the Kingdom. This is taken up by his disciple St. Paul, although because of the different context in which he taught, Paul is obliged to substitute the concept of "the Household" for that of "the Kingdom". Chapter Six continues the study of New Testament literature, with particular reference to the contributions of James and Luke. In contrast to Paul and some of the other writers, these contend that the economic life of a follower of Jesus must be characterised by disinvestment, poverty, and dependence on others.

Chapter Seven is concerned with three, early types of reaction by Christians to questions of economic organization and activity. One reaction is the communistic style of the primitive Christian community in Jerusalem. Another is the retreatism advocated by the Carthiginian-Roman lawyer, Tertullian. A third is the support of active engagement in existing economic structures by the Alexandrian teacher, Clement.

The remainder of the book is devoted to the new climate for patristic economic thinking that was engendered by the accession of Constantine and his legitimation of Christianity within the Roman Empire (A.D. 313). In Chapter Eight some of the currents of thought and action associated with this change are reviewed. Then, there is a treatment of the emergence of the Solution by Charity, which is identified, in particular, with St. Basil the Great, and of the Solution by Communism, associated with St. John Chrysostom (Chapter Nine). Turning to the West, the analysis continues with an examination of the views of St. Ambrose of Milan (Chapter Ten). Finally (Chapter Eleven), the thought of St. Augustine of Hippo is considered with special reference to his understandings of production and distribution, and to modern controversy on whether or not Augustine might have envisaged the possibility of economic growth and progress.

This study has been many years in its preparation, and has benefitted from the comments of a wide range of scholars associated with many universities. However, special thanks are due my friends and colleagues at the University of Newcastle (New South Wales). Some of these have provided invaluable intellectual stimulus and material support over a very long haul. In particular, I wish to thank my wife, Dr. Moira Gordon (Economics), Mr. Darryl Palmer and Professor Godfrey Tanner (Classics), and Dr. David Dockrill (Philosophy).

The typing of the manuscript was undertaken by secretarial staff in the Department of Economics, University of Newcastle. The devotion and efficiency of Mrs. Joan Allridge and Mrs. Lorraine King are acknowledged with gratitude.

> For man's character has been moulded by his everyday work, and the material resources which he thereby procures, more than by any other influence unless it be that of his religious ideals; and the two great forming agencies of the world's history have been the religious and the economic.
>
> Alfred Marshall, *Principles of Economics*

CHAPTER ONE

SCARCITY, FAITH AND WISDOM

> "Accursed be the soil because of you. With suffering shall you
> get your food from it every day of your life. It shall yield you
> brambles and thistles, and you shall eat wild plants. With
> sweat on your brow shall you eat your bread, until you return
> to the soil, as you were taken from it."
>
> *The Book of Genesis* 3:17-19

The initial exploration of the nature and origins of the economic problem in biblical literature is mainly attributable to the Yahwist. This author (or, group of authors) is also responsible for the exposition of certain of the strategies that might be adopted to cope with that problem. Most probably, the Yahwist wrote during the reign of Solomon in Judah (c. 965-926 B.C.), or a little later. He brought together much of the then current lore concerning primeval history in a new and powerful synthesis.[1] Because of its sharp, analytical thrust, the synthesis has remained a remarkably potent influence in the evolution of ideas across the centuries.

For this early writer, there is no doubt that the problem of scarcity is an ever-present burden for the bulk of mankind. Nature is not especially beneficent, and the acquisition of the means of life is a task involving continual struggle and personal cost. Such sentiments are not uncommon in surviving examples of other early ancient writings, and they may be compared, for example, with those of the Greek poet, Hesiod (c. 700 B.C.).[2] However, the Yahwist's treatment of scarcity has a distinctive character in that it involves the idea that humanity was not designed originally to be subject to the pressures involved. Further, the treatment denies that work is a feature of the human condition which is exclusively engendered by the pressures of scarcity. This latter is in marked contrast with the Greek tradition on the question.[3]

---

[1] C.f., G. von Rad, *Genesis, a Commentary* (London: S.C.M, 1972), pp. 16-17.

[2] On Hesiod, see, B. Gordon, *Economic Analysis Before Adam Smith: Hesiod to Lessius* (London: Macmillan, 1975), pp. 2-7.

[3] In the Greek tradition, work is, "the most oppressive misfortune that Zeus imposes upon men from their very birth." (Homer, *Iliad*, 10, 71). Work is a type of punishment, and nothing else.

SCARCITY AND WORK

The origins of the economic problem, according to the Yahwist, are located in the Fall of Man. Originally, the Creator ordained that the means of life should be freely available:

> "Yahweh God caused to spring up from the soil every kind of tree, enticing to look at and good to eat... Then Yahweh God gave man this admonition, 'You may eat indeed of all the trees in the garden. Nevertheless of the tree of the knowledge of good and evil you are not to eat for on the day you eat it you shall most surely die.' " (Gen. 2:9, 16).

This situation alters radically when mankind chooses to try to capitalise on the most distinctive attribute with which it has been endowed, i.e., the gift of the ability to disobey its Creator. Instead of remaining satisfied with the beneficence of Yahweh, humans decide to take control of the entire range of their choices as consumers of the fruits of creation. In Yahwistic terms, Adam and Eve eat the forbidden fruit (Gen. 3:1-6).

Since men and women have decided to care for their own welfare as far as consumption is concerned, there is no way in which Yahweh can honour that choice except by freeing them from their former state of dependence as consumers.[4] They must leave Eden if they are to live as they have chosen. They have taken upon themselves the problem of scarcity, a problem which it was not intended they should be obliged to face.

Given that mankind is not designed to cope with its chosen independence, it might be expected that this form of creation would quickly disappear from the face of the earth outside Eden. However, this is not the case. The reason is that these creatures were designed to be workers and were invested with the ability to innovate. They were not intended for an existence of idle enjoyment of the Creator's largesse in Paradise. Rather, they were made in the image of the God who works. Humans were settled in the Garden, "to cultivate and take care of it." (Gen. 2:15, see also, 2:5).

Work precedes the Fall and the onset of scarcity. For the Yahwist, its basic rationale is not the satisfaction of the worker's needs as a consumer. Instead, its chief significance is in its fulfilling an ordinance of God which relates to man's very being. This point has been observed by a variety of modern commentators among whom is Alan Richardson. He finds that the Yahwistic texts,

---

[4] Von Rad comments (op.cit., p. 97) that here, man has, "stepped outside the state of dependence, he has refused obedience and willed to make himself independent." On this and the related themes, consult the outstanding analysis by, C. Westermann, *Creation* (London: S.P.C.K., 1974), esp., pp. 80-90, 100-103.

"Do not represent work as coming into being as a result of sin but as part of the very intention of God in making the world and man... Apart altogether from sin and the Fall, man has work to do; he has a function to perform within the created order.."[5]

There is no doubt that in Eden, although its economic viability is not in question, mankind has responsibilities. Humanity has a job to do. The Yahwist uses terms such as "to cultivate" and "to take care of", and these are, "technical terms used frequently for the service of God and observance of the commandments. They express responsibility, the burden of man faced with the divine initiative."[6] Mankind is "burdened" in Paradise. It is confronted with the phenomenon of "cost".

Man the Worker is designed to cope with the burden of opportunity cost, i.e., a foregoing of the benefits of the outcomes of the possibilities discarded in the series of choices which a work process may entail. His position is analogous to that of the Creator when he set about his work. The character of man's burden is illustrated graphically by the Yahwist through the episode of the naming of the beasts:

"So from the soil Yahweh God fashioned all the wild beasts and all the birds of heaven. These he brought to man to see what he would call them; each one was to bear the name the man would give it. The man gave names to all the cattle, all the birds of heaven, and all the wild beasts." (Gen. 2:19-20).

This, it is obvious, is no mean task. In fact, so the Yahwist suggests, this challenge to work like God is so severe that man alone (Adam) is granted a "helpmate". With this equally endowed co-worker, the formerly singular image of God forms "one body" (Gen. 2:20-24).

After the Fall, mankind is not denied its role of sharing in God's work. Hence, it continues to incur opportunity cost. However, because of the choice to become independent as consumers, men and women subject themselves to a second type of cost. This is "real cost", in the sense of toil, physical pain, and sweat (Gen. 3:17-19). By embracing scarcity, humanity burdens itself beyond the intention of the Creator.

INNOVATION AND MERCY

By the end of the third chapter of *Genesis*, the Yahwist has presented his readership with a very bleak assessment of the human condition and of what they can expect in their lives. Nevertheless, even within that

---

[5] A. Richardson, *The Biblical Doctrine of Work* (London: S.C.M., 1958), pp. 25-26.
[6] A. Schökel, quoted in, Peter F. Ellis, *The Yahwist: the Bible's First Theologian* (London: Chapman, 1969), p. 186.

chapter there are some glimmers of hope. In the first instance, Adam and Eve do not die on the day they eat the forbidden fruit. Further, it would seem that Yahweh is not prepared to leave them entirely to their own devices in their self-elected contest with scarcity. Discovering the need for a new type of consumption item, clothing, the first pair's somewhat meagre innovation is the loin-cloth of fig leaves (Gen. 3:7). This is a weak response to independent assessment of need, so Yahweh provides a superior substitute, clothes made out of skins (Gen. 3:21).

Immediately after the departure from Eden there is another sign of hope. The "soil" may be "accursed" because of Adam (Gen. 3:17), but this does not preclude population growth (Gen. 4:1-2). Again, in the tale of Cain and Abel the Yahwist endeavours to demonstrate at length how the merciful intervention of God is available to give rise to benefits despite, and even through, the disasters evoked by the fledgling innovations of mankind. The fundamental innovation, in this case, is the division of labour: "Abel became a shepherd and kept flocks, while Cain tilled the soil." (Gen. 4:2). This arrangement leads to competition and then to fratricide. Abel loses his life, and the murderer Cain is rendered incapable of productive activity. Yahweh tells Cain:

> "Now be accursed and driven from the ground that has opened its mouth to receive your brother's blood at your hands. When you till the ground it shall no longer yield you any of its produce. You shall be a fugitive and a wanderer over the earth." (Gen. 4:11-12).

The full weight of this sentence is tempered by God's mercy. Cain is given a special mark to prevent his being murdered in his wanderings, and the upshot is a series of striking innovations. The descendents of Cain cannot cope with scarcity by means of tilling the soil, but this handicap gives rise to a wide range of new productive pursuits:

> "Cain had intercourse with his wife, and she conceived and gave birth to Enoch. He became the builder of a town... Adah gave birth to Jabal: he was the ancestor of the tent-dwellers and owners of livestock. His brother's name was Jubal: he was the ancestor of all who play the lyre and the flute. As for Zilla, she gave birth to Tubal-cain: he was the ancestor of all metalworkers, in bronze or iron." (Gen. 4:17-22).

Here, out of a crime associated with a simple division of labour has come a much more complex division which would not have eventuated without Yahweh's forebearance. It can be remarked also that the process of economic development implied by the narrative is observed to be grounded in the denial of traditional pursuits to "Cain's descendants." Development, it is suggested, is born of adversity.

The next narrative in the Yahwistic sequence is that of the Flood and Noah. This offers yet further affirmations that contemporary humanity does not experience the full economic implications of the Fall. Immediately after the Fall the soil became accursed (Gen. 3:17), but after the Flood, in the Covenant with Noah that marks the beginning of a new world order, Yahweh declares:

> "Never again will I curse the earth because of man... As long as earth lasts, sowing and reaping, cold and heat, summer and winter, day and night shall cease no more." (Gen. 8:21-22).

If the Yahwist can be interpreted in 3:17 as contending that mankind's struggle with scarcity is due in part to a fall of Nature together with Man, then 8:21-22 suggests that he also wished his audience to appreciate that this situation pertained only before the Flood. In any event, it is clear that the readership is to understand that the element of conflict between man and soil is greatly reduced after the Covenant with Noah. Perhaps, it is a token of the reduction that Noah is associated with a distinctive innovation. He is, "the first to plant the vine". (Gen. 9:20).

They may be part of a new world order, but the Yahwist does not want his contemporaries to gain the impression that they can innovate with impunity. Hence, as a final cautionary tale from primeval history he introduces the episode of the Tower of Babel. This is another occasion for the merciful intervention of God to save mankind from the adverse consequences of misdirected use of its powers. Just what the adverse consequences may be is by no means clear on this occasion.

In the Babel story, humanity (or, part of it united in Babylonia) comes together for a major co-operative enterprise. Yahweh, however, subverts the project by upsetting the ability of the workers to communicate. He decides to "confuse their language" (Gen. 11:7), and the builders are scattered over the face of the earth. God is portrayed as foreseeing that this particular enterprise is a prelude to an upsurge of further innovation: "This is but the start of their undertakings. There will be nothing too hard for them to do." (Gen. 11:6). In some unspecified manner, it is this circumstance which threatens adversity.

THE SOLUTION BY FAITH: ABRAHAM

Up to this point in the analysis, man has not dealt very well with his self-imposed task of combatting the pressures of scarcity. Despite man's capacity for innovation, the direct intervention of Yahweh has been necessary to promote the degree of development which has been achieved since Adam and Eve confronted the soil outside the Garden. Such a reflection on primeval history prepares the way for the Yahwist to show

how his readership can cope successfully. The Solution comes in the transition to patriarchal history when Abraham is called and elected.

The Yahwist's Solution is the Solution by Faith. It involves the precise reversal of the process which evoked scarcity in the first place. Adam and Eve opted for independence. In its beginning, mankind disobeyed a command which did not appear to make sense. By contrast, Abraham obeys a command which does not appear to make sense. Noah, it is true, anticipates Abraham in that he was willing to involve himself in the seeming absurdity of constructing a queer kind of ship in the midst of dry land. This proved decisive for the future of mankind. Abraham's decision is to prove crucial for the Jewish people, at least, and he is the more significant model for them.

God tells Abraham to leave one of the main, regional centres of civilisation and economic activity (Haran, or perhaps, Ur) for an unspecified destination, and Abraham accepts the command (Gen. 12:1-4). This is extraordinary since "to leave home and to break ancestral bonds was to expect of ancient men almost the impossible."[7] In the new life that his act of faith has opened up, Abraham and his dependents prosper. He is portrayed as travelling around the Middle East. Early on in his new career, after an eventful trip to Egypt, he is said to become, "a very rich man, with livestock, silver and gold." (Gen. 13:2).

This affluence, however, is not attained without cost, and a substantial cost is incurred in his initial act of faith. The act required his taking up sojourning. It required a positive response to, "the radical demand of God that the way of faith requires leaving a land and accepting landlessness as a posture of faith."[8] An even more radical demand (in the eyes of the Yahwist's audience) is made by God at a later date. Abraham is commanded to deny himself posterity as well as the ownership of land. He is to kill his only son Isaac (Gen. 22:2). The man of faith begins to commit himself to this ultimate in irrationality, but his hand is stayed by God's messenger and he is promised a well-nigh limitless posterity. In addition, the economic success continues unabated. Near the end of Abraham's life, his chief-steward can declare: "Yahweh has overwhelmed my master with blessings, and Abraham is now very rich. He

---

[7] G. von Rad, op.cit., p. 161.

[8] Walter Breuggemann, *The Land: Place as Gift, Promise and Challenge in Biblical Faith* (Philadelphia: Fortress, 1977), p. 6. Perhaps, for ancient man, the acceptance of landlessness is tantamount to accepting that there will be no reward for his taking on the burden of the problem of work. There will be no opportunity for dominion such as the role of Adam in his innocence afforded. The cost of forsaking the possibility of dominion, in Abraham's case, is reduced by the promise of land for himself or his descendents in some indefinite future. The extent to which this is a reduction depends on the degree of Abraham's attachment to the hope that the promise will be fulfilled.

has given him flocks and herds, silver and gold, men slaves and women slaves, camels and donkeys." (Gen. 24:35). There is circulating capital in abundance here. Still, the prize of land is unattained. There is only the promise (Gen. 13:17, 15:18).

THE SOLUTION BY WISDOM: JACOB AND JOSEPH

The abundance of Abraham continues with his son, Isaac (see, Gen. 26:13). The same comes to apply to Isaac's second son, Jacob, who eventually, "grew extremely rich, and became the owner of large flocks, with men and women slaves, camels and donkeys." (Gen. 30:43). Nevertheless, with Jacob, a new element enters into the strategy for overcoming the threat of scarcity. That element is Wisdom.[9]

Jacob, in his youth, is depicted as a reflective person who is by no means a man of action to rival Esau, his twin, who was first-born. Yet, through judgement of persons and circumstances, and with the aid of his mother, he secures both the birthright and blessing that custom required should be bestowed on Esau. These machinations make it prudent for him to exile himself with his mother's relatives. There, in exile, he becomes rich through exercising extraordinary managerial skill as a herdsman and breeder (Gen. 30:32-43). Subsequently, he skilfully negotiates a treaty with his irate father-in-law, Laban, and placates his brother Esau in another display of adroit diplomacy.

In the sphere of wisdom, however, the wily Jacob comes to be far outshone by "the son of his old age", Joseph. Whereas the figure of Jacob anticipates the ideal of the era of Solomon, the figure of Joseph embodies it. With Joseph we are given, "a good example of the goal toward which all training and education in Israel during the royal period directed a young man of good standing."[10]

The boy sold into slavery rises to become grand vizier of Egypt, and in the court story which details his agrarian policy he emerges as the consultant administrator without peer (Gen. 47:13-26). Joseph manipulates the tools of macroeconomic policy to deal with the onset of scarcity on a grand scale. He combats the problem wtih success, while also serving the interests of his ruler. As a *political* economist, his skill is such that at the end, Pharoah has come to own almost the entire country, but the populace gladly acclaim the administrator: "You have saved our lives.

---

[9] "Wisdom" is used here with reference to the meaning it had in earlier biblical literature. From the late pre-exilic period that meaning began to alter. On the contrast between old and new wisdom, consult William McKane, *Proverbs, A New Approach* (London: S.C.M., 1970), p. 648. See, also, G. von Rad, *Wisdom in Israel* (London: S.C.M., 1972), p. 317.

[10] G. von Rad, *Genesis, A Commentary* (London: S.C.M., 1972), p. 376.

If we may enjoy my lord's favour, we will be Pharaoh's serfs." (Gen. 47:25).

Apart from its celebration of economic policy-making as an exercise in Wisdom, this story is striking in its schematic presentation, attention to the detail of policy, and attempt to show the functional relationships of the steps involved. As von Rad has perceived, "the narrative betrays clearly a theoretical interest ... there pervades the narrative a naive pleasure in the possibilities of human wisdom which can conquer economic difficulties by a venturesome shift of values, money for bread, manpower and land for seed corn, etc."[11] Joseph begins by levying a tax in kind (corn) during years of abundance when the impost is likely to be least unpopular and do minimum damage to national welfare. The corn is put in government stores around the country (Gen. 41:33-36). Then, with the advent of famine in Egypt and elsewhere, Joseph commences selling the grain at home and abroad (Gen. 41:53-57). As the dearth continues, he eventually comes to command the total money supply on behalf of Pharoah, and, with no money, the populace is obliged to begin exchanging real capital (livestock) for corn (Gen. 47:13-17). Joseph, of course, has the grain to support the livestock.

Subsequently, their livestock gone, and with nothing else left to barter for grain, the Egyptians are reduced to trading their land for bread (Gen. 47:18-22). Pharaoh, through Joseph, now owns all the money, all the livestock, and all the land. The people have survived the famine, but at the expense of a wholesale transfer of property to the ruler. From now on, they will be serfs on Pharaoh's land, and Joseph allocates seed to them on the basis of a return of a fifth of the produce of every future harvest to the state (Gen. 47:23-24).

There is nothing else in the Old Testament to match this story, and both its character and setting raises the question of whether something approaching economic analysis was taught in the wisdom schools of Egypt long before the Greeks took their first steps along such a path with the Sophists. There is even a possibility that the practice could have applied for a time in Jerusalem. In Solomon's day, "an Egyptian-trained and perhaps Egyptian-staffed bureaucracy (1 Kgs. 4:1 ff) kept the books and provided the matrix for the kingdom's intellectual class."[12]

THE SOLUTION BY FAITH: MOSES

Thanks to Joseph's high status and diplomatic skill, Israel (i.e. Jacob, his family, and possessions) is able to give up its sojourning and is settled in

---

[11] ibid., pp. 409-410.
[12] P. F. Ellis, op.cit., p. 58. See also, W. McKane, op.cit., pp. 8-10.

the land of Goshen, the fertile Nile delta region. There the Israelites prosper and their numbers increase. However, there is a change in the ruling dynasty of Egypt, and the new king knows "nothing of Joseph." Presumably, no Wisdom figure has emerged among the Israelites to represent their interest effectively. They become prey to enslavement and attempts at genocide. (Ex. 1:8-22).

Moses is called by God to rescue his people. He is not a man in the mould of a Joseph or Jacob. Early in his career he kills an Egyptian for striking a Hebrew, a reaction that one can more readily associate with an Esau (Ex. 2:11-12). The Yahwist goes on throughout the text of *Exodus* to demonstrate the absence of an affinity with Wisdom on Moses' part. For example, Moses lacks eloquence and needs Aaron as his mouthpiece. Yet, skill with the spoken word is one of the chief hallmarks of the man of wisdom. Even more to the point, perhaps, is the episode in the desert in which Moses agrees to the appointment of judges to administer justice (Ex. 18:13-27). Such administration, in the era of Solomon, was central to the activities of the Wisdom adept.[13] Moses, however, is readily persuaded that overinvolvement in this type of work detracts from the performance of his major tasks: representing the people before God and teaching the people God's laws (Ex. 18:19-20).

Much of the emphasis in post-Yahwist writing is on the second of these tasks. Moses is the great law-giver who is commanded by God to issue a range of directives which is astonishing in terms of its breadth and its grasp of what will be the requirements of even the day-to-day minutae of righteous living in the Canaan which Moses never enters. With the Yahwist, on the other hand, the representative role has, at least, an equal weight. Moses represents his people before God, as did Abraham before him. Again, like Abraham, he is able to undertake this pre-eminent role because he is a man of extraordinary Faith. Moses' great strength is his willingness to listen. "Moses, Moses", calls Yahweh from the burning bush. "Here I am", Moses replies. (Ex. 3:4). His "Here I am" remains, despite the occasional momentary lapse on his part, as the recurring factor which sustains Israel. The people find their way to God primarily through the Faith of Moses, and not primarily through the Law he transmits. If Moses is the model, the Law is not at the centre of the God-Man relationship. Rather, it is a gift in aid of those who have not yet come to be able to listen.[14]

---

[13] Consult, John Gray, *I and II Kings, A commentary* (London: S.C.M, 1970), p. 101.

[14] This is not to deny the antiquity of Mosaic Law or a crucial role in its development by an historical Moses. On these issues, consult W. A. Albright, *Yahweh and the Gods of Canaan* (London: Athlone Press, 1968), pp. 143-159.

Moses, then, is not a figure to be cited in favour of the Solution by Wisdom which had been embraced by so many of the intelligentsia among the Yahwist's contemporaries. Nor, for the Yahwist, is he the archetypal exponent of the Solution by Observance of the Law such as some later Jewish writers portray him. Rather, as a man of faith, he is identified with a radical extension of the Solution associated with Abraham.

This radical extension is evoked by the contrast between the circumstances of Abraham and those of Moses. Abraham is the head of a sojourning family. Moses leads a polyglot band of wanderers. Obviously, there is the difference between a family and a group of escaping slaves, but more is involved. As Walter Breuggemann points out: "The wanderer is different from the sojourner-pilgrim because he is not on the way to anywhere. He is in a situation where survival is the key question".[15] For Moses and his wanderers in the desert, it is not a question of: prosperity, versus, the common condition of man after Noah. Instead, it is a question of: outright defeat in the contest with scarcity today, versus, living with the expectation of the probability of defeat when tomorrow comes.

In these circumstances, the Solution by Faith as the recourse for the people of God is expressed in forthright terms that the related emphases of patriarchal history only foreshadow. The wanderers are sustained by water from the rock (Ex. 17:1-7), they are fed manna from the heavens (Ex. 16:4-5, 14-15), and "a wind from Yahweh" brings quails (Num. 11:31-35). From these quite unexpected quarters, their extremity is relieved when Moses, in his faith, listens to God, and God, in his turn, listens to Moses. In the desert, there is no "soil" and no city, but the Israelites survive without the aid of either.

---

[15] W. Breuggemann, op.cit., p. 8.

CHAPTER TWO

OBSERVANCE OF THE LAW

"Listen to these ordinances, be true to them and observe them, and in return Yahweh your God will be true to the covenant and the kindness he promised your fathers solemnly. He will love you and bless you and increase your numbers; he will bless the fruit of your body and the produce of your soil, your corn, your wine, your oil, the issue of your cattle, the young of your flock, in the land he swore to your fathers he would give you. You will be more blessed than all peoples."

The Book of Deuteronomy 7:12-14

By far the most durable of the general solutions of the Old Testament for success in dealing with the economic problem is the Solution by Observance of the Law. The basic idea is that the people of God will prosper or languish in accord with its degree of conformity to a set of legal prescriptions. This novel departure is associated with the notion that the people of God now possess a Land and are no longer wanderers, guest workers, or sojourners. The key to sucess in the Land is meticulous observation of a Code embracing even the most minute facets of daily life. Faith and Wisdom are relegated to the background. The new outlook is expressed most emphatically in the *Book of Deuteronomy*, and it is continued in the *Book of Leviticus*.

The New Solution

The scenario for the emergence of the Deuteronomic solution is written in vivid tones by the classical prophets of the eighth century. The writings of Amos, Hosea, Micha and the first Isaiah accuse both Judah and Israel of apostasy and moral degradation. They rail at the trend to increasing concentration of ownership and control of resources. This has led to widespread exploitation of the mass of the populace.[1] In addition they perceive threats to the traditional worship of Yahweh from without and within the community. As Edward Neufeld has observed: "The monarchy, owing to its nature and to its effects, was the most radical

---

[1] Concerning the trend to concentration, see, Otto Kaiser, *Isaiah 1-12, a Commentary* (London: S.C.M., 1977), pp. 65-66; J. L. Mays, *Micha, a Commentary* (London: S.C.M., 1976) p. 64; and, H. W. Wolff, *Joel and Amos, a Commentary* (Philadelphia: Fortress, 1977), pp. 89-90.

revolution in ancient Israel. It aimed to give Israel an international status: to assimilate its governmental system, its economy and its cultural orientation to those of the contemporary neighbours.''[2] The foreign contacts and foreign models, as encouraged by the kings, pose an external threat. Even more serious than this are the inroads of the home-grown worship of Baal, son of the god of grain, provider of all fertility, and god of vegetation.

After the fall of the Northern Kingdom, and with increasing dissatisfaction among the people of Judah, there was an increased willingness of the powerful to take the prophets seriously. Reformers pressed for revitalisation of existing law, and for a centralization of the cult of Yahweh which would eliminate the confusion of worship sustained by the country shrines. About 622 B.C., King Josiah responded to the pressure, and a major reformation was set in train.[3] Much of the thought which informed that reformation is expressed in the *Book of Deuteronomy*.

The Book contains a new Code of Law which represents an outstanding effort at humanising contemporary society. The Code is set firmly in the Mosaic tradition, and some fifty percent of its ordinances are derived from the earlier Code of the Covenant. However, it is more comprehensive than the latter, and it insists on a new approach to the solution of the problem of scarcity, namely, Solution by Observance of the Law. Deuteronomic authors tend to treat the Solution by Faith rather as a relic of a by-gone era. For example, the author of the *Book of Joshua* (late seventh, or early sixth century, B.C.) writes that when the Israelites crossed the Jordan and entered the Promised Land: ''From that time, from their first eating of the produce of that country, the manna stopped falling. And having manna no longer, the Israelites fed from that year onwards on what the land of Canaan yielded.'' (Jos. 5:10-12). It was Faith in the desert and in the time of sojourning. It is Law in the Land. The way to prosperity, like the way to God, is now through the Law of Moses rather than through his Faith (or Abraham's).

Given the novelty of their approach, it is not surprising that the authors of *Deuteronomy* feel obliged to reiterate their Solution. With repeated emphasis the Book attaches to the Code the promise that the community or the individual adhering to its statutes will not know

---

[2] E. Neufeld, ''Socio-Economic background of Yobel and Semitta'', *Revista Degli Studi Orientali*, 33 (1958), p. 104.

[3] For the sequence of steps in the reformation, consult, J. Gray, *I and II Kings, a Commentary* (London: S.C.M., 1970), pp. 721-725, and J. Bright, *The Anchor Bible: Jeremiah* (N.Y.: Doubleday, 1965), pp. XXXVIII-XLV. An important recent study of some of the consequences of the reformation is, Morris Silver, *Prophets and Markets: the Political Economy of Ancient Israel* (Boston: Kluwer-Nijhoff, 1983).

deprivation. There are numerous passages with this import.[4] The theme is developed even further by the blessings and curses of Chapter 28 which concludes the second discourse. According to these, if the conquerors of Canaan obey the Law, they will experience population growth, capital expansion, favourable seasons, abundant output, political security, and inter-national dominion (Dt. 28:1-14). On the other hand, failure to keep the Law will result in economic disaster, plague, political subservience, and slavery to foreigners (Dt. 28:15-46). Some examples from the ''blessings'' passages are indicative. These read:

> ''You will be blessed in the town and blessed in the country. Blessed will be the fruit of your body, the produce of your soil, the issue of your livestock, the increase of your cattle, the young of your flock. Blessed will be your pannier and your bread bin ... Yahweh will summon a blessing for you in your barns and in all your undertakings, and will bless you in the land that Yahweh is giving you ... Yahweh will give you great store of good things, the fruit of your body, the fruit of your cattle and the produce of your soil, in the land he swore to your fathers he would given you. Yahweh will open the heavens to you, his rich treasure house, to give you seasonable rain for your land and to bless all the work of your hands. (Dt. 28:3-12).

The significance of these passages for subsequent Jewish, and even Christian, thinking proved profound. The agonised wrestling with the problem of the prosperity of the wicked in later Old Testament thought is just one manifestation of their impact. It was to be a long time before a new, alternative solution to the economic problem—the Trito— Isaiah's Solution by Mediation—was to be plainly articulated. Despite its manifest empirical invalidity, the deuteronomic solution has had an extraordinarily long life.

Priestly Reinforcement

The last set of major contributors to the *Pentateuch*, and those who brought it to its final form, were the writers in the priestly tradition (P).[5] These edited the earlier documents, commented on them, and added fresh material. Probably, much of this work was undertaken during the main years of exile in Babylon (587-538 B.C.), but it was begun before then and continued for a time thereafter.

In the Priestly Tradition the Solution proposed by Deuteronomy remains dominant. Hence, the *Book of Leviticus* affirms: ''If you live

---

[4] See, e.g. Dt. 4:40; 6:1-3; 6:14-19.

[5] Groups of contributors to the *Pentateuch* are conventionally designated as P, D, J and E, where these letters indicate: the priestly tradition (P); the deuteronomic school (D); Yahwistic sections (J); and, Elohistic passages (E).

according to my laws, if you keep my commandments and put them into practice, I will give you the rain you need at the right time; the earth shall give its produce and the trees of the countryside their fruits; you shall thresh until vintage time and gather grapes until sowing time. You shall eat your fill of bread and live secure in your land." (Lv. 26:3-5). At times, P appears to wish to go further than the Deuteronomists, and apply the new Solution in retrospect to Abraham. Priestly additions to *Genesis* include the suggestion that Abraham was a wealthy man *before* his decisive act of faith (Gen. 12:5). Again, he is told by God to "bear yourself blameless in my presence" if he is to hope for great increase in his posterity (Gen. 17:2). Also, the J theme of the cost of landlessness, a crucial aspect of the earlier solution, is muted by repeated returns to the idea that the patriarchs built in Canaan (see, e.g., Gen. 17:8; 28:4, 36:7; 37:1).

The priests subsume the Solution by Faith within their vision of the overriding importance of the Law. This is illustrated vividly by the way in which they go about explaining how scarcity will not present a special problem in the Sabbatical and Jubilee years when the land lies unsown and unharvested (Lv. 25:1-22).[6] It might be thought that the absence of economic difficulties is ensured as God's response to the act of faith which such a radical abandonment to his providential care requires. But this is not so. It is the demonstration of the willingness to obey the Law on Sabbatical and Jubilee (as given to Moses in the desert) which is the operative factor (see especially, Lv. 25:18-22).

The contrast between the traditional faith emphasis and the innovation by D and P is brought out clearly in the next chapter of *Leviticus* (Chapter 26). This contrast has been noted by Martin Noth, and his remarks are applied equally to the twenty-eighth chapter of *Deuteronomy*. He writes:

> "It must be admitted that this juxtaposition of blessings and cursings is in some tension with the Old Testament saying that God's blessing was freely vouchsafed to Israel, quite independently of Israel's prior obedience. The gift of the land, for example, which, along with its produce, plays a considerable part in the blessings and cursings announcement, was the fulfilment of a divine promise made without preconditions: it did not need to be earned by Israel as a 'reward' and could only be forfeited by unfaithfulness."[7]

---

[6] The details of the Law concerning Sabbatical and Jubilee are of particular interest for the historian of economic thought. On these, and related aspects of the Law, see B. Gordon, "Economic Welfare and Regulation of the Economy in the Pentateuch and the Mishnah", *Humanomics*, Vol. 1, No. 3 (1985), pp. 107-120.

[7] M. Noth, *Leviticus, a Commentary* (London: S.C.M., 1965), p. 197.

As with D, the priestly tradition allows little or no role for the Solution by Wisdom. Certainly, the latter tradition waxes lyrical over the skills of the craftsmen who build and furnish the Sanctuary (Ex. 25-31; 35-40). However, it is most doubtful that their efforts can be considered as manifestations of Wisdom. Even the Wisdom writers themselves, whether old or new, are most reticent concerning the status of the skill of craftsmen. This reticence is due, in large measure, to a desire to avoid any suggestion which might be construed as support for idolatory, the worship of the works of men's hands.[8] This point aside, P is emphatic that in the case of the Sanctuary it is a matter of Divine guidance from first to last: "Bezalel and Oholiab and all the skilled craftsmen whom Yahweh had endowed with skill and perception to carry out all that was required for the building of the Sanctuary, did their work exactly as Yahweh had directed." (Ex. 36:1).[9]

It must be remarked, however, that although the foregoing analysis of P has stressed its affiliations with D, it is not the case that the economic thought of the priests remains within the Deuteronomic framework entirely. The two traditions are at one on the question of Observance of the Law versus Faith and Wisdom. Nevertheless, P opens up new vistas for Jewish thinking on economic relationships. These vistas arise from: fresh insights concerning the possibilities for economic growth; a new universalism; and, a renewed probing of the meaning of work. Perhaps a good deal of this stemmed from what the priests in exile, and their fellows, found in Babylon.

Priestly Initiatives

One of the most striking aspects of the priestly tradition is the degree of economic rationalism which its contributors felt constrained to bring to the editing of existing accounts of patriarchal or national history. An instance of this is P's explanation of why Abraham and Lot went their separate ways: "The land was not sufficient to accommodate them both at once." (Gen. 13:6). P employs the same explanation to account for the separation of Esau from his brother Jacob (Gen. 36:6-8). Again, a later editor which could be P (but might be D) has Yahweh offering an economic basis for his policy of not permitting the Israelites a rapid con-

[8] C.f., A. Richardson, *The Biblical Doctrine of Work* (London: S.C.M., 1958), pp. 18-19.

[9] Post-biblical Jewish writers in the Talmudic tradition, by contrast, explored the Wisdom implications of the construction of the Sanctuary at length. On this see, R. A. Ohrenstein and B. Gordon, "Human Capital Issues in Talmudic Literature", *International Journal of Social Economics* (1987).

quest of Canaan. The conquest is to be allowed to proceed with a careful eye to its effects on the maintenance of a desirable population-to-land ratio. Yahweh reasons: "I shall not drive them [the existing inhabitants] out before you in a single year, or the land would become a desert where, to your cost, the wild beasts would multiply. Little by little I will drive them out before you until your numbers grow and you come into possession of the land." (Ex. 23:29-30).[10] *Deuteronomy* presents the same argument, but in an abbreviated form which omits reference to the multiplication of wild beasts as a function of the growth in the proportion of waste land. It also fails to refer to the lag in the response of population growth, which growth, *Exodus* appears to relate to the transition from the nomadic life to settled agriculture. (See, Dt. 7:22).

The population-to-land ratio is also well to the fore in the priestly version of God's instructions to the invading clans of Israel as to how they are to apportion the territory they win. Shares are not to be determined by valour in battle or by the chances of campaign. Rather, "To the large in number you are to give a large area of land, to the small in number a small area; to each the heritage will be in proportion to the number registered. The dividing of the land is, however, to be done by lot." (Nb. 26:54-55; see also, 33:54). From this it would seem that to the priests, population size was the rational criterion for allocation of extent of area. However, they refrain from giving a rationale for determining the relative geographical situations of the areas.

Population growth is an obvious concern for the priestly editors of J and E, and they associate achievement of this goal with economic development in the sense of increasing freedom from the vagaries of natural forces. This same concern is present in *Leviticus*. What were welcome manifestations of God's blessing for J and E are transformed by the priests into divine ordinances for man. Hence, in P's version of primeval history, Adam and Eve are told to increase their numbers and gain control of their environment: "Be fruitful, multiply, fill the earth and conquer it." (Gen. 1:28).[11] These same imperatives are presented to Noah in an expanded form (Gen. 9:1-7). The new emphasis is carried on into patriarchal history. The contrast between the P version of the blessing of Jacob by Isaac (Gen. 28:3-4) and the J version (Gen. 27:27-29) is indicative of the change in outlook.

---

[10] Brevard Childs comments that this passage, "is being offered to explain why in fact the conquest did not succeed in eradicating the Canaanite population." B. S. Childs, *Exodus, a Commentary* (London: S.C.M., 1974), p. 487.

[11] On the significance of this verse for the biblical doctrine of work, see John Paul II, *Laborem Exercens* (Australian edition; Sydney: St. Paul, 1981), pp. 20-22.

In accord with their general approach to the problem of scarcity, the priests suggest that Israel will enjoy growth and development if there is strict observance of Mosaic law by the community. Given the latter, the Law of Holiness predicts that increasing numbers and a recurring annual surplus of output will go hand-in-hand: "If you live according to my laws, if you keep my commandments and put them into practice ... I will turn towards you, I will make you be fruitful and multiply, and I will uphold my Covenant with you. You shall eat your fill of last year's harvest, and still throw out the old to make room for the new." (Lv. 26:3-10).

The economy of Israel, then, is to be anything but stagnant if the community adheres to the detail of its covenant obligations. *Deuteronomy* appears to share this view when it predicts, "you will be creditors to many nations and debtors to none." (Dt. 15:6). However, there is less evident concern with growth in this latter tradition.

ECONOMIC GROWTH AND THE LAW

Given the presence of a conditional promise of growth and development in the priestly writings, the question arises as to whether or not the laws promulgated by the priests were helpful for Israel's realization of the promise. Was the goal to be looked for compatible with the life-style recommended for the law-abiding? The findings of a number of modern commentators suggest that it was not. Rather, the laws, in their opinion, had a decidedly anti-growth bias. Concerning that bias Edward Neufeld writes that institutions such as jubilee, debt-release, and sabbatical were attempts, "to safeguard the preservation of old socio-economic forms by regularly repeating a new economic programme and thus arresting and suppressing the development of city life and its economy."[12] Neal Soss states: "The interdiction of the rational use of capital, the land transfer mechanism, and the jubilee all serve to maintain the agrarian society of small holders created at the Conquest. The same forces also result in a relatively slow rate of growth of income."[13]

Against such assessments, it is possible to cite features of the evolution of Mosaic law which were encouraging for growth. Some of these features are: promotion of monetisation of the economy; increasing regard for strangers; and, the emergence of an overt economic

---

[12] E. Neufeld, "Socio-Economic Background of Yobel and Semitta", *Revista Degli Studi Orientali*, Vol. 33 (1958), p. 118.
[13] N. M. Soss, "Old Testament Law and Economic Society", *Journal of the History of Ideas*, Vol. 34 (1973), p. 343.

rationalism in association with secularization of cultic arrangements.[14] Not only *Leviticus*, but *Deuteronomy* also contains such features. Monetisation in the interest of centralization of worship is a key factor, but there are other pro-growth elements in the deuteronomic code. One of these is a wide-ranging humanism which is supportive of enhanced social mobility. A vivid illustration of the latter is the new status accorded women. As Moshe Weinfeld points out:

> "In contrast to the earlier Biblical sources, in which no mention is made of women and according to which the male participants in covenant ceremonies must even separate themselves from their women before the ceremony (Exod. 19:15), the author of Deuteronomy makes a particular point of mentioning that women, as well as men, participate (29:10 and 17; c.f. 31:12). The same is true of the festivals and the festal repasts. On such occasions we meet with the Israelite's daughter as well as his son, and his maidservant as well as the manservant (12:12 and 18; 16:11 and 14)."[15]

Another factor emphasised in *Deuteronomy* is the secure status of personal possessions. For example, where debtors are concerned (Dt. 24:10-13):

> "Deuteronomy further protects the debtor ... by forbidding the lender to march into the house of the debtor as though he owned the place. He must wait at the door and (probably, before witnesses) receive the pledge which the debtor had chosen. This sensitive enlargement of the ancient law is distinguished by the deuteronomist's categorial style."[16]

Security of property, like opportunity for social mobility, is a prime influence on the degree of economic enterprise which is likely to be present in any community.[17] It cannot be said then, that after *Leviticus* and *Deuteronomy* the face of the Law was set unequivocally against the

---

[14] Concerning these features, see, B. Gordon, "Biblical and Early Judeo-Christian Thought: Genesis to Augustine", in, S. Todd Lowry (ed.), *Pre-classical Economic Thought* (Boston, Kluwer, 1987), pp. 49-53.

[15] M. Weinfeld, *Deuteronomy and the Deuteronomic School* (Oxford: Clarendon Press, 1972), p. 291.

[16] E. W. Heaton, *The Hebrew Kingdoms* (Oxford: Oxford University Press, 1968), p. 229. The type of "sensitive enlargement" to which Heaton refers is seen by some writers as mainly a reflection of an earlier golden age. H. Eberhard von Waldow, for example, writes of "the earlier period of social equality and equal opportunities" in which the enlightened nomadic or semi-nomadic "paterfamilias" presided over communities in which "private property is never used to oppress the neighbour" and, "tried by all means to avert" the spread of poverty. See H. Eberhard von Waldow, "Social Responsibility and Social Structure in Early Israel", *Catholic Biblical Quarterly*, Vol. 32 (1970), pp. 182-204. In the light of the Bible's own version of the history of the Hebrews, one may be permitted to doubt the existence of a golden age and a regression thereafter. For example, compare Deuteronomy on warfare (Dt. 20:1-4; 20:19-20; 21:10-14) with accounts of the Conquest.

[17] It can be added that Dt. 22:1-3 makes provision for the care and return of lost property.

economic development of Israel. However, it may be that the Law helped structure the economy so that certain types of growth were more likely to occur than others. Perhaps, it even fostered a dualistic economy where the potential for change was much greater in one set of sectors than elsewhere.

Dualism is a feature of the less developed economies of the second half of the twentieth century A.D. In these economies there are sectors of activity which are akin to their counterparts in more developed economies. They are characterised by higher levels of personal income, greater emphasis on secular education, and greater mobility of persons and property than is found in the sectors where traditional practices rule. Often, the dichotomy is most obvious when urban-associated activities are contrasted with those based in rural areas.

The Law in ancient Israel seems to favour non-rural pursuits, in that entrepreneurs engaged in these are not subject explicitly to the same variety of constraints as that surrounding the sale, purchase, and use of land. Again, such entrepreneurs may not have been subject to the same degree of taxation as were rural producers. In *Deuteronomy*, for example, there is insistence on the custom of an annual tithe of rural produce. The Book is silent on the subject of an equivalent obligation for other producers or for rentiers. By far the clearest illustration in the Law of an urban-rural dualism is given by *Leviticus*. The Law of Holiness recognises and sanctions the existence of two kinds of economy where the purchase and sale of houses is concerned. The context is the legislation relating to jubilee and redemption. Leviticus states: "If anyone sells a dwelling house that is in a walled town, he shall have the right of redemption until the expiry of the year following the sale. His right of redemption is limited to the year; and if the redemption has not been effected by the end of the year, this house in the town shall be the property of the purchaser and his descendents in perpetuity; he need not relinquish it at the jubilee. But houses in villages not enclosed by walls will be considered as situated in the open country; they carry the right of redemption, and the purchaser must relinquish them at jubilee." (Lv. 25:29-31).

Here, it is not the type of commodity itself but the socio-economic setting of its sale which is decisive. It is one law for the city, and another for the village. Transfer of capital according to commercial practice is to be subject to greater constraints in rural as against urban areas.

In this as in other respects, the agricultural sector is given over to more explicit containment in terms of covenant obligation than others.[18]

---

[18] Probably, one of the reasons for the greater degree of containment was the fact that agriculturalists were traditionally prey to moneylenders.

Enterprising Jews who are also intent on perfect observance of the Law, have an excellent incentive to get out of entanglements with the Land. The rural economy is dominated by a fundamental principle: "The heritage of the sons of Israel is not to be transferred from tribe to tribe; every man of the sons of Israel is to remain bound to the heritage of his patriarchal tribe." (Nb. 36:7). No prospect of economic gain, whether individual or communal, can be permitted to over-ride obedience to the implications of this rule.

CHAPTER THREE

THE SOLUTION BY MEDIATION

> "Strangers will be there to feed your flocks, foreigners as your
> ploughmen and vinedressers; but you, you will be named
> "priests of Yahweh', they will call you 'Ministers of our
> God'. You will feed on the wealth of nations and array
> yourselves in their magnificence."
>
> *Isaiah* 61:5-6.

After the Babylonians completed their seige of Jerusalem and destroyed
the first Temple, they began a series of deportations of the local
inhabitants from 597 B.C. It would seem that those selected for deporta-
tion included most of the Jewish intelligentsia and skilled tradesmen (see,
2 Kgs. 24:14-16; and, Jr. 24:1). With its human and its mobile, physical
capital plundered, the Judean economy was prostrate. In addition, it is
probable that the administration of law and order was far from conducive
to economic recovery. According to *Lamentations*: "Slaves rule us; no one
rescues us from them. At the peril of our lives we earn our bread, by risk-
ing the sword of the desert." (Lm. 5:8-9).

It is not surprising that exilic and post-exilic biblical literature includes
among its concerns an exploration of the pre-conditions for a revival of
the economy of Judah. The later prophets figure prominently in the
debate.[1] However, most of these offer no new departure with respect to
the economic problem as a general issue. Scarcity will be overcome by
observance of the Law. Nevertheless, there is an emergence of fresh
insights, some of which eventually crystallized as, The Solution by
Mediation. According to this Solution, Israel will prosper if its people act
as intermediaries between God and the members of other nations.

JEREMIAH AND ISAIAH

The first hint that the economic welfare of the Israel of the future will
turn on its adopting a mediatory role is to be found in the writings of
Jeremiah. In a pamphlet which he addressed to the exiles in Babylon, he
advised:

---

[1] On this aspect of later prophetic writings, see, B. Gordon, "Economic Dimensions
of the Revival of Israel in the Thought of the Later Jewish Prophets," in, C. Tisdell
(ed.), *Contributed Economic Essays: A Collection in Memory of Dr. M. G. Kibria*, Newcastle:
Department of Economics, 1987.

"Build houses, settle down; plant gardens and eat what they produce; take wives and have sons and daughters; choose wives for your sons, find husbands for your daughters so that these can bear sons and daughters in their turn; you must increase there and not decrease. Work for the good of the country to which I [Yahweh] have exiled you; pray to Yahweh on its behalf, since on its welfare yours depends." (Jr. 29:5-7).

This advice outraged one of the exiles, who wrote to Jerusalem that, "in the case of a madman who acts the prophet, your duty is to put him in the stocks and iron collar." (Jr. 29:26). The outrage is understandable since, as John Bright comments, "a command to Jews to pray for the hated heathen power is otherwise unexampled in literature of the period."[2] It was revolutionary to suggest that the captives should mediate between God and their captors as part of the means of restoring Israel. The revolutionary sentiment was never entirely suppressed thereafter, although the old Law-theme continued to more than hold its own.

Mediation begins to take on a higher profile in sections of the *Second Isaiah*. This prophet (or, prophetic school) has the most sanguine expectations concerning what the new Israel can be. At the centre is the city of Jerusalem as an outstanding complex of conspicuous affluence, intellectual activity, and material well-being:

"Unhappy creature, storm-tossed, disconsolate,
see, I will set your stones on carbuncles
and your foundations on sapphires.
I will make rubies your battlements,
your gates crystal,
and your entire wall precious stones.
Your sons will all be taught by Yahweh.
The prosperity of your sons will be great."
(Is. 54:11-13).

Surrounding the City, there is a resurgent rural economy which is even able to permit re-afforestation (Is. 32:15). The corn harvests will be rich, and animal-feed will be abundant (Is. 30:23-24). Small country towns will be revived (Is. 44:26).

The wholesale restoration seems to have little to do with the Solution by Wisdom. In fact, the Second Isaiah associates the wise men with charlatans: "I [Yahweh] am he who foils the omens of wizards and makes fools of diviners, who makes sages recant and shows the nonsense of their knowledge." (Is. 44:25). The restoration also appears to be unrelated to

---

[2] J. Bright, *The Anchor Bible: Jeremiah* (New York: Doubleday, 1965), p. 211.

the professional interests of the priests.[3] Solution by Observance of the Law is even less in evidence.

Given his suspicion of wisdom and his relative unconcern for the specifics of the Law, it is not entirely out of character that the Second Isaiah emphasises the role that the Solution by Faith must play in economic recovery. To this end, he undertakes to revive reflection on the archetypal man of faith, Abraham. He asks his compatriots:

> "Consider the rock you were hewn from,
> the quarry from which you were cut.
> Consider Abraham your father
> and Sarah who gave you birth.
> For he was all alone when I called him,
> but I blessed and increased him.
> Yes, Yahweh has pity on Zion,
> has pity on all her ruins;
> turns her desolation into an Eden,
> her wasteland into the garden of Yahweh."
> (Is. 51:1-3).

The emphasis on the role of Faith is continued in 55:1-3, where the Israelites are invited to, "buy corn without money, and eat, and, at no cost, drink wine and milk." Here, as John McKenzie perceives, "food and drink are not mere metaphor..."[4]

Given the neglect of the patriarchs by the pre-exilic prophets, this revival of the Solution by Faith in the writings of the Second Isaiah can be regarded as a considerable innovation.[5] It is a significant retrospective element in his thought and opens up much wider horizons than those contemplated by either Jeremiah or Ezekiel.

Up to this point, the Second Isaiah has jettisoned: Wisdom; priestly concern with centralised cultic ritual surrounding the Temple; and, the old attempt at setting a Law at the centre of the life of the people of God. Only Abraham and his Faith have survived the onslaught. The ground-clearing exercise prepares the way for the emergence of the idea of a cosmopolitan "Israel" whose welfare is bound up with the work of an unprecedented figure, "the Servant."

The horizons of Jewish thought are greatly extended in the Servant Songs.[6] By any standards, these are remarkable contributions to the

---

[3] C.f., J. L. McKenzie, *The Anchor Bible: Second Isaiah* (New York: Doubleday, 1968), p. 74.

[4] ibid., p. 143.

[5] C.f., Claus Westermann, *Isaiah 40-66: a Commentary* (London: S.C.M., 1976), p. 236.

[6] The songs comprise: Is. 42:1-9; 49:1-6; 50:4-9; and, 52:13-53:12. These may be the work of Deutero-Isaiah, but this is a debateable point.

history of ideas, although their authorship is uncertain and their meaning
remains controversial. Much of the controversy centres around the figure
of the Servant. In the opinion of Christopher North: "The Prophet may
have intended to describe Israel, but his final portrait is that of the perfect
Israelite."[7] Some scholars would go further, and find in these songs the
first, clear sketch of the figure of a personal Messiah.[8]

The writer of the Songs is not especially concerned with prediction of
the shape of the future economy of Israel-in-the-Land. In fact, in his
view, the idea of the Land and the idea of Israel have only a peripheral
relationship. Hence, the restoration of Israel is bound up with a process
that goes well beyond the borders of one area of the Near East. On his
plane of vision: "Israel is not 'saved' merely by being re-established as
a community or even as a kingdom. Its destiny goes much farther than
this."[9] The Yahweh of these songs is not merely the God of the covenant
with Moses' band. Rather, he is the Creator who has regard for all his
creatures and desires that the nations have "light" (Is. 42:5-7).

The revival of Israel's fortunes is depicted as part of the outcome of
the work of the Servant, but it is only a part:

> "And now Yahweh has spoken,
> he who formed me in the womb to be his servant,
> to bring Jacob back to him,
> to gather Israel to him:
> 'It is not enough for you to be my servant,
> to restore the tribes of Jacob and bring back the survivors
>   of Israel.
> I will make you the light of the nations,
> so that my salvation may reach to the ends of the earth.' "
> (Is. 49:5-6)[10]

No preconditions are stated for what might be done to ensure the advent
of the Servant, and there is no indication of any means of facilitating his
work. It might be presumed that what is required is a period of watchful
expectation followed by one of full obedience to the Servant when he
comes. However, this is just presumption, especially as the fourth song
predicts that the Servant will be despised, rejected, and killed (Is.
53:2-9).

This preceding thought sets the stage for the classic statement of the
Solution by Mediation in the Third Isaiah. The set of writings involved
is probably from the late sixth or early fifth century B.C., and once again

---

[7] C. R. North, *The Second Isaiah* (Oxford: Clarendon Press, 1964), pp. 20-21.

[8] See, e.g., Charles C. Torrey, *Ezra Studies* (New York: Ktav, 1970), p. 314.

[9] J. L. McKenzie, op.cit., p. xlviii.

[10] "These verses seem to place a clear antithesis between the Servant and
Jacob/Israel." ibid., p. 104.

Jerusalem is at centre stage as the prime manifestation of the results of the optimal economic strategy. The City is to become the focal point of an international outpouring which establishes it as a pinnacle of civilized affluence. In a restored Israel, the populace will enjoy "the wealth of the nations" and, "the riches of the sea." There will be an abundance of camels, sheep, incense, gold, silver, and rare woods. In fact, the people will be, "designed for beauty." The vision is expressed at length in *Isaiah* 60:1-22. There is, in sum, "remarkable prominence given in Trito-Isaiah's picture of the future salvation to the economic and the material ... the prophetic proclamation contains a considerable element of accept-ance of the refinements of civilization."[11]

What are the bases for this triumph over scarcity? Two of the bases represent direct acknowledgement of the humanistic aspects of *Deuteronomy* and the importance of the role of cultic practice (*Leviticus*). In establishing the pre-conditions for the affluence, Trito-Isaiah puts great emphasis on the achievement of social justice. The prophet, himself, claims that he has been sent, "to bring good news to the poor, to bind up hearts that are broken; to proclaim liberty to captives, freedom to those in prison." (Is. 61:1-2). In his new society, workers will not be oppressed by their masters, the homeless will be sheltered, the hungry given bread, and the naked clothed (Is. 58:3-12). A second, prominent pre-condition is observation of the sabbath (Is. 56:2; 58:13-4; 66:23).

However, the third basis goes well beyond traditional deuteronomic and levitical thought. It involves an attempt at specification of the cosmopolitan role envisaged for Israel by the Second Isaiah (see above). As John McKenzie writes, with the Third Isaiah,

> "A different conception of Israel and the nations which come to Zion is pro-posed. Israel had been presented as the mediator between Yahweh and the nations; that position is here defined as the priesthood, which in Israel had the office of offering sacrifice and prayer in the name of the people and pre-senting and explaining the law of Yahweh. Israel will have no concern with its material needs as the Israelite priesthood theoretically had no concern with these needs. The nations of the world will support Israel in its mission of mediation."[12]

Israel, then, solves its economic problem by priestly mediation on a global scale. The prophet is quite explicit on the point. He writes:

> "Strangers will be there to feed your flocks,
> foreigners as your ploughmen and vinedressers;
> but you, you will be named 'priests of Yahweh',

---

[11] C. Westermann, op.cit., p. 362. See also, J. L. McKenzie, op.cit., p. lxix.
[12] ibid., pp. 181-182.

> they will call you 'ministers of our God.' You
> will feed on the wealth of nations and array
> yourselves in their magnificence.''
> (Is. 61:5-6).

This new Solution, it must be acknowledged, is only achieved at the expense of abandoning the idea of "Israel" which informed the deuteronomic reform and the efforts of the priestly scholars. Now, the communal point of reference is a society in which foreigners and even eunuchs who acknowledge Yahweh are fully fledged members of ''the people'' (Is. 56:3-8). The term ''Israel'' denotes a global association of peoples whose adherents are not confined to those whose ancestors passed through the Desert and occupied plots of land in Caanan. With this Isaiah, ''the new community is on the way to a new form of association which is no longer identical with the old concept of the chosen people.''[13] The old concept is most emphatically rejected in the following: ''I am coming to gather the nations of every language. They shall come to witness my glory. I will give them a sign and send some of their survivors to the nations: to Tarshish, Put, Lud, Mashech, Rosh, Tubal, and Javan, to the distant islands that have never heard of me or seen my glory. They will proclaim my glory to the nations. As an offering to Yahweh they will bring all your brothers ... and some of them I will make priests and Levites, says Yahweh.'' (Is. 66:18-21).

It would also seem that the new strategy concerning scarcity is associated with the evolution of a theology emphasising the universal fatherhood of God (Is. 64:7-8). Such is the fatherhood of God, that it renders insignificant considerations relating to human paternity. Isaiah puts the genealogical preoccupations of many of the earlier writers in their place, as follows: ''Do not let your compassion go unmoved, for you are our Father. For Abraham does not own us and Israel [i.e. Jacob] does not acknowledge us; you, Yahweh, yourself are our Father, Our Redeemer is your ancient name.'' (Is. 63: 15-16).

In the light of the foregoing, it is understandable that no weight is given to restoration of the Temple as a pre-condition of economic and social recovery. Prophets such as Haggai and Malachi (see, e.g. Hg. 1:9-10, 2:15-19; Ml. 3:9-11) are very concerned with the revival of this old institution. By contrast, Isaiah asks: given the true nature of Yahweh, how could any group of his creatures hope to capture him in a particular physical environment? Isaiah writes:

> Thus says Yahweh:
> With heaven my throne

---

[13] C. Westermann, op.cit., p. 314.

and earth my footstool,
what house could you build me,
what place could you make for my rest?
All of this was made by my hand
and all of this is mine—it is Yahweh who speaks.''
(Is. 66:1-2)

JOB

The theme of contesting scarcity successfully through mediation is not confined to the school of Isaiah. Outside the realms of prophetic literature, the theme asserts itself in *The Book of Job*. In contrast with the prophets, the authors of *Job* do not arrive at the Solution by Mediation by concentration on the issue of what the future Israel could be. Rather, they take up a scandal surrounding the Law. The confident catalogues of blessings and curses in *Deuteronomy* do not seem to have held in reality. The contributors to *Job* reflect on the deprivation of the virtuous.

The idea that those who are truly devoted to God may be required to undergo an unusual degree of suffering is not entirely absent in early Jewish thought. The outstanding instance in this regard is the command to Abraham to deny himself posterity by the immolation of his son (Gn. 22:1-19). However, the idea is expressed with increased emphasis in later centuries.

The misfortunes of a life dedicated to the will of Yahweh are a striking feature of the anguished ''confessions'' of Jeremiah (see especially, Jr. 20: 14-18). In these, the prophet questions his very existence: ''Why ever did I come out of the womb to live in toil and sorrow and to end my days in shame?'' (v. 18). A similar note is sounded in the ''Book of Consolation'', which is attributed to the Deutero-Isaiah. Here, the suffering servant of Yahweh is rewarded by,

''a grave with the wicked,
a tomb with the rich,
though he had done no wrong
and there had been no perjury in his mouth.
Yahweh has been pleased to crush him with suffering.''
(Is. 53:9-10).

An extensive treatment of this theme is undertaken in the *Book of Job*. There is general agreement that this book represents the classic discussion of the deprivation of the virtuous. There is agreement too on the challenge it offers to both *Deuteronomy* and the type of Yahwistic piety evident in the post-Deuteronomic material of the *Book of Proverbs*. That material, William McKane observes, ''provides the point of departure for the questionings of Job and the scepticism of Ecclesiastes."[14]

At the outset of the book, and at numerous points thereafter, it is made clear that Job has been a perfect observer of the Law. From the relevant verses we gain a vivid appreciation of the conventional ideals concerning the character, life and status of such an individual.[15] Job represents conventional morality at its best. In him, as Norman Snaith writes, we have, "an excellent picture of what Deuteronomic theory envisaged as the state of the truly pious and perfect man."[16]

The drama begins when this paragon is plunged into the depths of a lingering deprivation short of death. His predicament then gives rise to a series of dialogues between Job and three "friends" who are probably business associates. Job had been an agriculturist on a grand scale by local standards. He had owned, "seven thousand sheep, three thousand camels, five hundred yoke of oxen and five hundred she-donkeys and many servants besides" (Jb. 1:3). To maintain this quantity of real capital, he must have engaged in extensive trading over a wide geographical area. When disaster strikes his enterprise, three of those connected with it journey to visit him.

Job's associates come from Idumaean and Arab territory. Eliphaz is from Teman, Bildad from Shuah, and Zopher from Naamath. As the dialogues proceed, each of these shows himself to be well schooled in the conventional wisdom which had found its way from other cultures into Israelite thought. As Marvin Pope notes: "The recovery of Mesopotamian Wisdom Literature now makes it clear that the position of the friends is essentially what was normative in Mesopotamian thought for centuries before Israel emerged in history."[17] This wisdom, like *Deuteronomy*, maintains that the just must triumph over scarcity, whereas the wicked must suffer a fate akin to that of Job.

Against the conventional diagnosis, Job sets two empirical realities: his personal record of unblemished righteousness, and the obvious thriving of the unjust. "Do we often see a wicked man's light put out, or disaster overtaking him, or all his goods destroyed by the wrath of God?", asks Job (21:17). As for himself, if he can get a hearing from God concerning

---

[14] W. McKane, *Proverbs, A New Approach* (London: S.C.M., 1970) p. 19. There is no general agreement on the authorship, literary origins or dating of *Job*. For a sample of divergent views consult W. F. Albright, *Yahweh and the Gods of Canaan* (London: Athlone Press, 1968), pp. 224-7; R. B. Y. Scott, *The Way of Wisdom in the Old Testament* (N.Y.: Macmillan, 1971), pp. 40-1; and G. Von Rad, *Wisdom in Israel* (London: S.C.M., 1972), pp. 207.

[15] See Jb. 1:1-5; 23:10-12; 27:5-6; 29:1-20; 31:1-34.

[16] N. Snaith, "The Prosperity of the Wicked," *Religion in Life*, 20 (1951), p. 521.

[17] M. H. Pope, *The Anchor Bible: Job* (New York: Doubleday, 1973), p. LXXVIII.

his conduct, he will give God an account of every step of his life and "go as boldly as a prince to meet him" (31:37).

By the end of the dialogue sections, the *Book of Job* gives the strongest impression that, despite the rationalisations of his friends, Job has sustained his case. Divine justice does not work as convention would have it. Both ancient wisdom and the Deuteronomic outlook are mistaken. Hence, it seems odd that in the Epilogue (Jb. 42:7-17) the fortunes of the righteous Job are restored. Scott, for example, finds this, "a result confirming the friends' arguments which Job in the poem has so emphatically denied."[18] Eugene Goodhart writes that, "the epilogue subverts the scepticism of the poetry by seeing to it that justice is done. Job's anguished claim that the virtuous are unrewarded and the vicious unpunished is, as it were, denied by the epilogue."[19]

Job's restoration as a person of even greater substance is attributed by many to multiple authorship of the work and/or the demands of literary convention.[20] However, another type of explanation is possible. Perhaps, the contradiction between Dialogue and Epilogue is more apparent than real. It can be contended that the Epilogue does not deny Job's rejection of the validity of the conventional approach. Rather, this section points to an alternate way to freedom from deprivation for the just.

Whether or not an alternate solution is presented in the Epilogue depends on the weight given the simple (and quite unambiguous) statement: "Yahweh restored Job's fortunes because he had prayed for his friends" (Jb. 42:10).[21] This statement seems to deserve weight, given Job's circumstances, who his friends were, and the reason for his praying. Reflection on these suggests that Job is restored by an act which combines faith, a willingness to serve the needs of others, and a cosmopolitan approach to the issue of who should be served.

As the Epilogue opens, Job is a man crushed in body, and routed in argument by Yahweh. Yet, here at the end, he remains a man of faith. His physical and intellectual capacities at the end of their tether, he does not will the non-existence of Yahweh. Instead, he is quick to take action when there is an opportunity to serve his friends (who, for the most part, have taken the role of accusers). The friends have incurred the anger of Yahweh, but Job can avert it by interceding for them. Further, in praying for these men, he is probably acting out of compassion for a group of "foreigners" (men outside the Covenant). Job is returned from

---

[18] R. B. Y. Scott, op.cit., p. 162.

[19] E. Goodhart, "Job and the Modern World," *Judaism*, 10 (1961), p. 22.

[20] Consult, e.g., R. D. Moore, "The Integrity of Job," *Catholic Biblical Quarterly*, 45 (1983), pp. 17-31.

[21] C.f., M. H. Pope, op.cit., p. LXXXI.

deprivation to plenitude by an act which implies a much more complex God-man relationship than the deuteronomists (and, perhaps, even the prophets) had discovered.

RUTH

The dramatic entry of the Solution by Mediation in the epilogue of *Job* sets the scene for an extensive exposition of that Solution's veracity in the *Book of Ruth*. Strong similarities between Job and Ruth have been noted by a number of commentators. Robert Gordis, for instance, writes that the author of Job, "is an exemplar of the universalism of spirit which existed in Second Temple Judaism side by side with more particularistic views. This attitude finds expression in the idyllic *Book of Ruth*, with its gentle insistence that nobility of character and faith in God are to be found among all human beings, Jew and Gentile alike."[22] However, the similarities go further, especially when it is recognised that Ruth derives its unity as a story from the course of the fortunes of the Job-like figure of Naomi, who is Ruth's mother-in-law.[23] Put briefly, it can be said that the Israelite Naomi is translated from extreme deprivation to joyful fulfilment by virtue of Yahweh's response to her mediation on behalf of a foreigner, the Moabitess, Ruth.

When the story opens, Naomi has lost her husband and both of her sons. She is left with the sons' Moabite wives, Orpah and Ruth. To add to her woes, she is in a foreign land and is now too old to find another husband. Faced with this desperate situation, she prays that Yahweh will intervene on behalf of the two young foreigners:

> "Go, return each to her mother's house.
> May Yahweh do with you the same kindness
> Which you have done for the dead and for me.
> May Yahweh give you recompense,
> In that you find security,
> Each in the home of her husband."
> (Rt. 1:8-9).[24]

Ruth does not return home, but accompanies Naomi to Bethlehem ("the house of bread") in Israel. There, Naomi mediates again by skilfully arranging a set of circumstances which lead to Ruth's marrying the upright and well-to-do Boaz (Rt. 3:1-5). Yahweh's response to this union is Ruth's conception and the bearing of a son. At this, there is general

---

[22] R. Gordis, *The Book of God and Man: a Study of Job* (Chicago and London: University of Chicago Press, 1973), p. 213.

[23] C.f., Edward F. Campbell, *The Anchor Bible: Ruth* (N.Y.: Doubleday, 1975), p. 168.

[24] This translation, and those which follow, are from E. F. Campbell, op.cit.

rejoicing in Bethlehem. The women of the town proclaim: "A son is born to Naomi!" The boy is her "redeemer", her "life-restorer", and the being who will sustain her through her old age (Rt. 4:13-17).

The "universalism of spirit" which suffuses this story is underscored by the contention that the boy, Obed, was none other than the grand-father of King David himself (Rt. 4:17-22). The consequent affirmation that the King's great-grandmother was a Moabite woman must have been a sore point indeed for those contemporary or later Jews who branded marriages between Israelite men and Moabite women as abominations.

The Solution by Mediation as proposed in the *Book of Ruth*, it must be emphasised, is not presented as effective without the presence of certain conditions. As for the school of Isaiah, there must be a turning of the foreigner to Yahweh. Early in the story, Ruth affirms: "For wherever you go, I will go; where you lodge, I will lodge. Your people become my people; your God is now my God." (Rt. 1:16). Again, as with the Isaiah tradition, there must be social justice in Israel. The figure of Boaz in the story of Ruth epitomises the reign of justice, and this is indicated by Rt. 2:8-12. Reflecting on these verses, Campbell writes: "The important thing to see here is that there is a distinct ingredient of good will, of will-ingness to help, indeed of determination to care for the widow and the destitute, which is fundamental to the Ruth story."[25] The figure of Boaz may be contrasted, in this respect, with that of the "near redeemer" in the legal episode at the city gate (Rt. 4:1-12). Unlike Boaz, the redeemer is only prepared to aid someone in difficulties as far as the law requires.[26]

There are hints in Ruth that the effectiveness of mediation may depend on pre-conditions other than social justice and an openness on the part of foreigners. For example, in her plan for the night at the threshing floor (Rt. 3:1-5) Naomi displays a craftiness worthy of a Jacob. Again, the effectiveness might turn on a willingness to forego the possession of ancestral land. The change in Naomi's fortunes is bound up with her willingness to sell a part of a field to which, it seems, she had some form of right of possession (Rt. 4:3-9).

Understood in its intellectual context, *Ruth* is no mere pastoral idyll. Some commentators have suggested that it is a deliberate protest against a rising tide of racial intolerance in post-exilic Jerusalem, and this may well be the case.[27] However, it is considerably more certain that the Book

---

[25] ibid., p. 110.
[26] C.f., ibid., pp. 158-9.
[27] C.f., Wesley J. Fuerst, *The Books of Ruth, Esther, Ecclesiastes, The Song of Songs, Lamentations* (Cambridge: Cambridge University Press, 1975) pp. 10, 30.

is an affirmation of the position that the future political and economic viability of Israel turns on an acceptance of the role recommended for the people of God by Jeremiah, Isaiah, and the epilogue of Job.

Scarcity, in this strand of Jewish thought, is a problem which demands for its solution a catholicity that those in Israel who thought their identity depended on observance of the minutae of the Law found impossible to accept. These latter, in the event, predominated. Catholicity was rejected in favour of even more elaborate exploration of the implications of the Law. As a matter of history, Israel was destroyed as a political and economic entity for many centuries. Whether *Ruth, Job*, and the insights of Jeremiah and the Isaiah tradition, if accepted, could have sustained the people of God in the Land as a viable national entity in economic and political terms must remain an unanswerable speculation.

CHAPTER FOUR

SCEPTICISM AND APOCALYPTIC

> "The words of Qoheleth son of David, king in Jerusalem.
> Vanity of vanities, Qoheleth says. Vanity of vanities. All is
> vanity! For all his toil, his toil under the sun, what does man
> gain by it?"
>
> *Ecclesiastes* 1:1-3.

> "For in those days and at that time, when I restore the for-
> tunes Judah and Jerusalem, I am going to gather all the
> nations and take them down to the Valley of Jehoshaphat;
> there I intend to put them on trial for all they have done to
> Israel, my people and my heritage."
>
> *Joel* 4:1-2.

As post-exilic Israel continued to languish in subject obscurity, impotent as either a political or economic force, the tensions posed by the contrast of this reality with what was popularly supposed to be the status of the chosen people of God gave rise to some reactions bordering on despair. Certain of the reactions which came to the brink of despair, but refused to plunge over it, constitute landmarks in the history of ideas. One of these landmarks is established by the urbane reflections of "the preacher" (Qoheleth). These reflections (*The Book of Ecclesiastes*) include an emphatic rejection of the belief in the existence of any general solution to the economic problem. A second landmark, the prophecies of Joel, signals the entry of a new perception in Jewish thought. Faith, Wisdom, the Law, or Mediation cannot singly or together prove decisive in the restoration of Israel. According to the new perception, only a decisive (apocalyptic) intervention by God himself will give Israel mastery in its contest with scarcity and the depredations imposed by surrounding peoples. *Qoheleth* and *Joel*, in their radically different ways, are both manifestations of a people near the end of its tether.

QOHELETH

Viewed from the perspectives of earlier biblical writing and of a deal that was come, *Qoheleth* is essentially a "ground clearing" exercise. In par-ticular, the author endeavours to purge Jewish thinking of some of the alien elements it had acquired during the centuries in the Land. He does not hesitate to give the lie to the deuteronomic Solution by Observance of the Law or to the old Solution by Wisdom. There are strong affinities

with the *Book of Job*. As Scott remarks: "...the authors of Job and
Qoheleth are wise men in revolt against the unexamined assumptions of
their colleagues."[1]

The empirical invalidity of the blessings and curses associated with
Deuteronomy are observed with a marked irony: "The sinner who does
wrong a hundred times survives even so. I know very well that happiness
is reserved for those who fear God, because they fear him; that there will
be no happiness for the wicked man and that he will only eke out his days
like a shadow, because he does not fear God. But there is a vanity found
on earth; the good, I mean, receive the treatment the wicked deserve;
and the wicked the treatment the good deserve. This, too, I say, is
vanity." (Qo.8:12-14). Elsewhere, he writes: "In this fleeting life of
mine I have seen so much: the virtuous man perishing for all his virtue,
for all his godlessness the godless living on." (Qo.7:15-16). The Solution
by Wisdom is given similar shrift: "I see this too under the sun, the race
does not go to the swift, nor the battle to the strong; there is no bread
for the wise, wealth for the intelligent, nor favour for the learned; all are
subject to time and mischance." (Qo.9:11).

Qoheleth also dismisses certain of the traditional ends or goals of
Jewish life as vacuous. He advises his readers to avoid concern with matters of posterity and geneaological succession (Qo.2:18-23; 4:14-16; 6:1-
3). Again, he discounts the notion that survival to an old age is a blessing
(Qo.12:1-8). The accumulation of capital in either real or monetary form
is another vanity. Even Solomon (with whom the author identifies, as a
literary fiction) found no ultimate satisfaction in his wealth (Qo.2:4-11).
Far from being a source of enjoyment, possession of capital gives rise to
personal cost (Qo.5:11). Beyond this, those who aim at accumulation
find themselves in a perpetual state of unsatisfied desire: "He who loves
money never has money enough, he who loves wealth never has enough
profit." (Qo.5:9, see also, 4:8). This portrayal of the capitalist mentality
by Qoheleth is the same as that of Aristotle, before him, and afterwards,
of Karl Marx.[2]

Adoption of any one of the above goals involves the individual in
attachment to future utilities. Against this, Qoheleth counsels that such
utilities should be discounted heavily. He advises concentration on
immediate experience which is necessarily ephemeral. Repeatedly, he
returns to the theme that eating, drinking, and working are the ends to
be sought by the rational man. These are the activities ordained by God

---

[1] R. B. Y. Scott, *The Way of Wisdom in the Old Testament* (New York: Macmillan, 1971),
p. 140.

[2] On the filiation of Aristotle and Marx, see, B. Gordon, *Economic Analysis Before Adam
Smith: Hesiod to Lessius* (London: Macmillan, 1975), pp. 36-37.

as the sources of human happiness (Qo.2:24; 3:12-13; 5:17-19; 8:15; 9:7).

Of particular interest here is Qoheleth's treatment of work as an end, rather than a means. "I see there is no happiness for man," he writes, "but to be happy in his work, for this is the lot assigned him." (Qo.3:22). This emphasis is not surprising, given the approach to work in the *Book of Genesis* (see, Chapter One). However, it is foreign to orthodox modern economic theory, and it is foreign to the mainstream of the ancient Greek tradition. For the Greek poet Hesiod, for example: "Work appeared in history simultaneously with the world's decline; the necessity of labour ... is a species of futility which became a burden upon mankind, in proportion as the world entered upon its period of decadence and was slowly plunged into an abyss of wretchedness."[3]

In accord with his attitude to work and his conviction that concentration on accumulation is debilitating, Qoheleth recommends that those who have capital should use it to facilitate entrepreneurship. To hold money, he allows, provides a measure of "protection" (Qo.7:12-13). However, the best course is to be willing to engage in risk. He argues: "Cast your bread on the water; at long last you will find it again. Share with seven, yes with eight, for you never know what disaster may occur on earth. When clouds are full of rain, they empty it out on the earth. Keep watching the wind and you will never sow, stare at the clouds, and you will never reap... For which will prove successful, this or that, you cannot tell; and it may be that both will turn out well together." (Qo.11:1-6; see also, 4:9-12).

This passage probably reflects the contemporary trading boom in Palestine which had been, "originated by that host of Greek officials, agents and merchants who flooded the land in the truest sense of the word and penetrated into the last village of the country."[4] It is likely that its author practiced what he preached. James Williams comments that the frequency of nouns signifying "profit" in Qoheleth, "probably points to a commercial environment in which trade has opened up and become a preoccupation of the sage's life situation."[5]

---

[3] Etienne Borne and Francoise Henry, *A Philosophy of Work* (London: Sheed and Ward, 1938), pp. 34-5. See also, Alan Richardson, *The Biblical Doctrine of Work* (London: S. C. M., 1958), p. 15.

[4] M. Hengel, *Judaism and Hellenism* (London: S. C. M., 1974), Vol. I, p. 43. *Qoheleth* was probably written between 270 and 220 B.C. In the immediate background were economic changes in Palestine facilitated by Ptolemaic rule.

[5] J. G. Williams, "What Does It Profit a Man?: The Wisdom of Koheleth", *Judaism*, 20 (1971), p. 185. C.f., M. J. Dahood, *Canaanite-Phoenician Influence in Qoheleth* (Rome, 1952).

Greek influence may be present also in Qoheleth's macroeconomic observation that growth and change depend on the presence of competition in society. He is at one with the poet Hesiod (and, with Adam Smith) in the statement: "I see that all effort and all achievement spring from men's mutual jealousy." (Qo.4:4). This view is consistent with his perception of the inefficiencies and dysfunctions of governmental bureaucracies. The bureaucratic organisation is not conducive to economic and social welfare: "If in a province you see the poor oppressed, right and justice violated, do not be surprised. You will be told that officials are under the supervision of superiors, who are supervised in turn; you will hear talk of the service of the king." (Qo.5:7-8).

This judgement of bureaucracy is very different from that of the deuteronomic *First Book of Kings*. In that Book, a detailed description of Solomon's bureaucracy concludes with enthusiasm: "Judah and Israel lived in security, each man under his vine and his fig tree, from Dan as far as Beersheba, throughout the lifetime of Solomon. Judah and Israel were like the sand by the sea for number; they ate and drank and lived happily." (1Kgs.4-5). For literary purposes, Qoheleth may have styled himself "son of David, king in Jerusalem", but it is clear that he was anything but enamoured of the figure of the historical Solomon. Despite his endowments, the latter chased vanities (Qo.2:4-11), and his bureaucratic regime did not improve the lot of the people as a whole.

Although he exposes the inadequacies of much earlier Jewish thought, and although he recommends a different life-style, Qoheleth is not prepared to advocate that alternative as a new general solution. "Who knows what is good for man in his life-time," he asks, "in those few days he lives so vainly, days that like a shadow he spends?" (Qo.6:12). The Solution by Observance and the Solution by Wisdom may be shams, but he cannot formulate a replacement.

One reason for Qoheleth's inability to go on from his critique is his exclusion of the possibility of any vision of salvation-history.[6] Man, he acknowledges, has been created for a purpose, and God has given him the ability to reflect on his temporal condition. But this is as far as it goes: "I contemplate the task that God gives mankind to labour at. All that he does is apt for its time; but though he has permitted man to consider time in its wholeness, man cannot comprehend the work of God from beginning to the end." (Qo.3:10-11; see also, 8:16-17).

Qoheleth longs for a glimpse of "the end", and, as von Rad has perceived, this wise man, "experiences the hiddenness of the future as

---

[6] C.f., M. Hengel, op.cit., p. 117.

one of the heaviest burdens of life.''[7] He is either incapable of undertaking, or unwilling to venture into, the type of historical exercise which is a feature of *The Wisdom of Solomon*.

Another reason for Qoheleth's lack of a general alternative is the faintness of his hope that there might be a meaningful existence for the individual after death. He does not seem to be entirely bereft of hope. Reflecting on the return of both man and beast to the dust, he speculates: "Who knows if the spirit of man mounts upward?" (Qo.3:21). This question seems to be answered in the affirmative near the end of his book when he writes that in death, "the dust returns to the earth as it once came from it, and the breath to God who gave it." (Qo.12:7). That part of man which is of God returns to God. Not too much, perhaps, should be read into such statements. Certainly, the idea of a meaningless afterlife is presented with greater vigour. "Whatever work you propose to do," he advises, "do it while you can, for there is neither achievement, nor planning, nor knowledge, nor wisdom in Sheol where you are going." (Qo.9:10). From this, it would seem that, for Qoheleth, the vanity of each and every life is founded on the futility of what follows, as well as on the hiddenness of the end of God's work in creation.

The biblical commentator on this book wrote: "Qoheleth tried to write in an attractive style and to set down truthful thoughts in a straightforward manner. The words of the sages are like goads, like pegs driven deep." (Qo.12:10-11). This is a very fair assessment of the place of this work in the development of biblical thought. Qoheleth confronted his contemporaries with some of the lacunae they continued to tolerate. Then, with determination, he began to pose certain of the questions which those who wished to argue the meaningfulness of life could not continue to avoid.

JOEL AND THE DAY OF YAHWEH

A very different reaction to the plight of Israel, as compared with that of Qoheleth, is represented by the prophecies of Joel. However, it is also an extreme reaction by comparison with preceding literature on economic and political revitalisation. Probably, the writings of Joel somewhat precede those of Qoheleth, and they may be a product of the first half of the fourth century B.C.

The main significance of *Joel* in terms of the development of thought on the economic problem is that of directing attention to the promise of an Ultimate Solution for the people of God, a solution depending on a

---

[7] G. von Rad, *Wisdom in Israel* (London: S. C. M., 1972), p. 234.

massive and decisive intervention by God in world history. It is through
this intervention that the righteous can hope for enduring relief from the
recurrence of the spectre of scarcity. As Leslie Allen observes: "Within
the confines of the O.T. revelation the prophecy of Joel reaches a high-
water mark of promise."[8] The prophet attains this mark through the
heightened employment of an old concept, the Day of Yahweh.

Joel seizes the opportunity to shake the complacency of his contemporaries when the Judean economy is brought to its knees by a combination of locust plague and drought. These phenomena were not unknown
in the region, but on this occasion the devastation seems to have been
particularly pronounced. He writes:

> "It has laid waste my vines
> and torn my fig trees to pieces;
> it has stripped them clean and cut them down,
> their branches have turned white.
> Wasted lie the fields,
> the fallow is in mourning.
> For the corn has been laid waste,
> the wine fails,
> the fresh oil dries up."
> (Jl.1:7, 10).

In the face of this, Joel issues a call to national repentance (Jl.2:12-17).
The people, it would seem, respond wholeheartedly, and Yahweh who
is, "jealous on behalf of his land" (2:18) takes pity on them. The
economy is restored to health. Once again, the soil is watered, beasts find
pasture, threshing floors are full of grain, and vats overflow with wine
and oil (Jl.2:21-17).

Most of this is not particularly remarkable in terms of biblical thought,
but then Joel goes further by claiming that the advent of the plague of
locusts marks the beginning of the coming of an ultimate intervention by
God. The plague, "by no means leads him to admonish the people to
listen to the voice of Yahweh in the Torah, as the Deuteronomists had
done. Instead, the calamity stimulates him to give heed to the unfulfilled
eschatological word about the Day of Yahweh ... The history of salvation
has not already reached its fulfilment in the cultus to which Joel so
matter-of-factly assents. A final convulsive event is still to come, namely,
that event which the prophetic word of the Day of Yahweh has
announced."[9] On and beyond (and transcending) the Solution by
Observance of the Law, there is another Solution.

---

[8] L. C. Allen, *The Books of Joel, Obadiah, Jonah and Micah* (London: Hodder and
Stoughton, 1976), p. 38.
[9] H. W. Wolff, *Joel and Amos* (Philadelphia: Fortress, 1977), p. 10.

The idea of the Day of Yahweh is present in earlier prohetic thought.[10] However, this prophet puts unprecedented emphasis on it. At this time, according to Joel, God will come in person to judge the nations of the world and to establish the truly enduring Israel. In the new order which ensues, although the lands of enemies will be deserts, the Land itself will be filled with abundance:

> "When that day comes,
> the mountains will run with new wine
> and the hills flow with milk,
> and all the river beds of Judah
> will run with water.
> A fountain will spring from the house of Yahweh
> to water the wadi of Acacias.
> Egypt will become a desolation,
> Edom a desert waste
> on account of the violence done to the sons of Judah
> whose innocent blood they shed in their country.
> But Judah will be inhabited for ever,
> Jerusalem from age to age.
> 'I will avenge their blood and let none go unpunished,'
> and Yahweh shall make his home in Zion."
> (Jl. 4:18-21).

Here, through the direct and definitive coming of Yahweh to make his home in Zion, the reign of scarcity in Judah will be ended. This Solution, it can be remarked, presents a considerable contrast with that of Isaiah's mediation strategy (Chapter Three). In the latter, Israel solves its economic problem without any suggestion that its gains have been achieved at the expense of direct costs to surrounding peoples. With Isaiah, Job and Ruth, there is even the implication that a priestly role by Israel among the nations yields mutual economic benefits all around. For Joel, the advent of a thriving Israel appears to involve, of necessity, the collapse of neighbouring economies.

APOCALYPTIC DEVELOPMENT

The type of desperation which surfaces in *Joel* continues on as a major, underlying theme in the subsequent, apocalyptic genre. Apocalyptic authors extended and universalized the concept of the Day of Yahweh. These writers display some affinities with some of the prophets, but the perspective on the process of socio-economic change is quite different. Concerning the difference, H. H. Rowley writes: "Speaking generally,

---

[10] Consult, G. W. Ahlstrom, *Joel and the Temple Cult of Jerusalem* (Leiden: Brill, 1971), pp. 62-97.

the prophets foretold the future that should arise out of the present, while the apocalyptists foretold the future that should break into the present."[11] The prophets were greatly involved in an attempt to spell out preconditions for national recovery, in terms of both individual and communal action. With the apocalyptists, on the other hand, that recovery is to be effected suddenly and at a pre-ordained time. Its occurrence will be quite independent of prior efforts concerning economic, political, or social policy. Apocalyptic writing, according to D. S. Russell,

> "is essentially a literature of the oppressed who saw no hope for the nation simply in terms of politics or on the plane of human history. The battle they were fighting was on a spiritual level; it was to be understood not in terms of politics and economics, but rather in terms of 'spiritual powers in high places'. And so they were compelled to look beyond history to the dramatic and miraculous intervention of God who would set to rights the injustices done to his people Israel."[12]

Recent scholarship has tended to push the origins of Jewish apocalyptic back as far as even the sixth century B.C.[13] This tendency has a deal to commend it, especially in that the writings concerned are set firmly in the understanding of salvation history which characterises the early books of the Old Testament. Nevertheless, there is no gainsaying the importance of the considerably less venerable Greek milieu. As Martin Hengel remarks, "no Jewish trend of thought borrowed so strongly from its oriental Hellenistic environment as apocalyptic."[14] The emergence of apocalyptic as a distinct genre in Jewish literature is associated with the intellectual currents and events of the Hellenistic period.

Alexander the Great died at Babylon in 323 B.C., and Ptolemy I took control over Jerusalem in 320 B.C. Under his successors there was active hellenisation in Palestine, and this was intensified when the territory came under the rule of the Seleucids after the Battle of Paneion in 198 B.C. The inroads of Greek culture were resisted by some elements of the Jewish people, and especially by the *Hasidim* or "pious ones". Conflict between the proponents of the two cultures reached breaking point when Antiochus IV Epiphanes (175-163 B.C.) desecrated the sanctuary of the temple in Jerusalem and launched a vigorous persecution of the anti-hellenists. One outcome was the Maccabean revolt. Another was the

---

[11] H. H. Rowley, *The Relevance of Apocalyptic* (London: Lutterworth, 1963), p. 38. Consult also, E. W. Nicholson, "Apocalyptic", in G. W. Anderson (ed.), *Tradition and Interpretation* (Oxford: Clarendon Press, 1979), esp. pp. 207-8.

[12] D. S. Russell, *The Method and Message of Jewish Apocalyptic* (London: S.C.M., 1971), pp. 17-8.

[13] See, E. W. Nicholson, op.cit., p. 211.

[14] M. Hengel, *Judaism and Hellenism* (London: S.C.M., 1974), p. 251.

appearance of apocalyptic in an emphatic form. The outstanding literary product was the *Book of Daniel.*

THE BOOK OF DANIEL

Daniel was written between 167 and 164 B.C. It is the only example of Jewish apocalyptic to find a place in the Hebrew canon. It also seems to have had a considerable impact on the terminology and outlook of some of the writers of the New Testament, despite the fact that most of these endeavoured to begin to dampen down the fervour concerning the imminence of the End which had been fueled by *Daniel* and similar writings.

Pre-ordained "times", together with marvellous events, are staples of the *Book of Daniel.* The Book also gives prominence to the faith and the devotion to the Law of particular Israelites. However, these latter serve as means of provoking the marvellous events and, more significantly, as necessary conditions for revelations of "times". Faith and Observance do not contribute to the emergence of new circumstances for Israel, but rather, help evoke the possession of knowledge that better days are certain to come.

Most immediate for the writer of *Daniel's* audience are the forecasts of his fourth "vision" (Chapters 10-12). These deal with the downfall of Antiochus IV and the age of prosperity and peace which will then dawn for the people of God. As with *Joel,* surrounding nations suffer during the advent of the new era. An aspect of the era, not present in *Joel,* is a resurrection of the righteous among the dead of former generations to join the living in the restored Israel. The forecast affirms:

> "At that time Michael will stand up, the great prince who mounts guard over your people. There is going to be a time of great distress, unparalleled since nations first came into existence. When that time comes, your own people will be spared, all those whose names are found written in the Book. Of those who lie sleeping in the dust of the earth many will awake, some to everlasting life, some to shame and everlasting disgrace. The learned will shine as brightly as the vault of heaven, and those who have instructed many in virtue, as bright as stars for all eternity." (Dn. 12:1-3).[15]

The appearance of the idea of resurrection in this passage is not an entirely isolated occurrence in terms of contemporary Jewish literature. For example, the second brother who is tortured to death in *2 Maccabees* exclaims: "Inhuman fiend, you may discharge us from the present life, but the King of the world will raise us up, since it is for his laws that we

---

[15] The "Michael" in these verses is the patron and guardian angel of the people of God.

die, to live again for ever." (2M.7:9). Nevertheless, the passage in *Daniel* marks in a particularly clear fashion the culmination of a lengthy process of evolution within Jewish thought.[16] Further, it sets a precedent for later, extrabiblical apocalyptic writing.[17] In addition, it anticipates a key idea of the New Testament.

The advent of the doctrine of resurrection as a widely-held belief signifies the presence of a new climate for thinking about the meaning of such mundane matters as economic activity. For example, it greatly reduces the degree of urgency which might be attached to the problem of explaining the temporal prosperity of the wicked and the deprivation of the just.[18] Reward and punishment become factors associated with the circumstances of a resurrected life in eternity. Economic success or failure as an individual or as a nation bear no necessary relationship to personal or communal integrity.

---

[16] C.f., D.S. Russell, op.cit., p. 356; Andre Lacocque, *The Book of Daniel* (London: S.P.C.K., 1979), p. 26; and, N. Porteous, *Daniel, a Commentary* (London: S.C.M., 1979), p. 19.

[17] For detail, consult, D.S. Russell, op.cit., pp. 368-372.

[18] In earlier Jewish literature, the *Psalms* offer extensive reflection on this issue. See, e.g., B. Hall, "The Problem of Retribution in the Psalms," *Scripture*, 7 (1955), pp. 84-92.

CHAPTER FIVE

THE KINGDOM AND THE HOUSEHOLD

> "So do not worry; do not say, 'What are we to eat? What are we to drink? How are we to be clothed? It is the pagans who set their hearts on all these things. Your heavenly Father knows you need them all. Set your hearts on his kingdom first, and on his righteousness, and all these other things will be given you as well."
>
> *Gospel of Matthew* 6: 31-33

Jesus of Nazareth (c.6 B.C.-A.D. 30) is the most important figure in the history of Western thought. His recommended general strategy for dealing with the economic problem is the Solution by Seeking the Kingdom. In the gospels, the strategy is enunciated most clearly during the Sermon On The Mount (Mt. 5-7; see also, Lk. 12, especially verses 22 to 32). Jesus' most active missionary disciple, Paul of Tarsus, proposed much the same solution except that given the political and social circumstances under which he preached, Paul substituted the concept of "the Household" for that of "the Kingdom".

THE SERMON ON THE MOUNT

At an early stage in the gospels of Matthew and of Luke, Jesus is confronted with the issue of what he is going to do about the phenomenon of scarcity. The confrontation occurs during the Temptation narrative (Mt. 4:1-11; Lk. 4:1-3), which narrative aims at, "enlightening the disciples on the nature of the Messiahship of Jesus and the methods appropriate to such a Messiahship."[1] Here, the devil challenges Jesus: "If you are the Son of God, tell these stones to turn into loaves". (Mt. 4:3). Jesus' reply makes it clear that he does not understand his mission as one involving the abolition of the burden of scarcity. He has not come to deny mankind its primeval choice of independence in this respect (see, Chapter One). Rather, he has come as part of the Father's response to man's choice. Jesus quotes *Deuteronomy* at the devil: "Man does not live on bread alone but on every word that comes from the mouth of God." (Mt. 4:4). Jesus' mission is orientated to life through the word.

---

[1] W. D. Davies, *The Sermon on the Mount* (Cambridge: Cambridge University Press, 1969), p. 74.

After this, in the Matthean sequence, Jesus hears that John the Baptist has been arrested, begins preaching, and calls the first four men who are to assist him in this work (c.f. Mk. 1:14-20). However, Jesus does not merely "proclaim the Good News of the Kingdom." He also sets about restoring dependent members of the community to a condition where they can better fend for themselves in the business of procuring their daily bread. Jesus cures, "all kinds of diseases and sickness among the people." (Mt. 4:23-25). This sets the scene for the Sermon on the Mount.

The opening chapter of the Sermon is about the character of the Father, and about living in terms of the kingdom. Much of the teaching is summed up by the concluding verse: "You must therefore be perfect just as your heavenly Father is perfect." (Mt. 5:48).[2] Then, Jesus moves on to teach his listeners how to pray (Mt. 6:9-13). This prayer—the "Our Father"—is also given in Luke 11:2-4.

Perhaps the most innovative feature of the prayer in terms of the history of ideas is offered by the probability that Jesus used the Aramaic term " 'abba" for "father" in reference to Yahweh. The significance of " 'abba" is that it affirms the existence of an intimate, filial relationship between the individual person and Yahweh. This affirmation, it should be remarked, seems to be even stronger in Luke than in Matthew since Luke uses the simpler form of address. Howard Marshall comments:

> "Jewish prayers referred to God as Father, but the simple form is not attested in Palestinian usage... The use of the intimate form was the amazing new thing that Jesus wished to teach his disciples, initiating them into the same close relationship with the Father that he enjoyed... The force of the term is to assure the disciples of God's loving care for them, so that they can ask him for gifts with the certainty of being heard."[3]

It is within the context of " 'abbâ" that the succeeding petitions of the prayer might be best understood, and these include the request: "Give us this day our daily bread" (Mt. 6:11, R.S.V.). Here, there is the suggestion that Yahweh will no more allow anyone who lives in terms of filial

---

[2] Consult, D. M. Stanley, *The Gospel of St. Matthew* (Collegeville, Minn.: Liturgical Press, 1963), pp. 41-2; A. H. McNeile, *The Gospel According to St. Matthew* (London: Macmillan, 1961), p. 73; and E. Schweizer, *The Good News According to Matthew* (London: S.P.C.K., 1978), p. 135.

[3] I. H. Marshall, *The Gospel of Luke* (Exeter: Paternoster, 1978), pp. 456-7. See also, E. Schweizer, op.cit., p. 149; and R. E. Brown, "The Pater Noster as an Eschatological Prayer", *Theological Studies*, 22 (1961), p. 183. The word " 'abba" is found twice in the epistles of Saint Paul. For comment, see C. K. Barrett, *A Commentary on the Epistle to the Romans* (London: Black, 1971), p. 163. The word is found also in the Gethsemane episode (Mk. 14:36). It should be noted that Vermes has claimed that the use of the Aramaic " 'abba" form with respect to God was not necessarily distinctive of Jesus. See, G. Vermes, *Jesus the Jew* (London: Collins, 1973), p. 210.

dependence on him to go hungry than would a caring father remain idle while his child starved. That this is the suggestion has been questioned by some biblical commentators in the recent past. These contend that the petition for bread should be understood in eschatological terms, i.e., as a petition for heavenly bread.[4] It has nothing to do with the economic problem. Yet, the eschatological interpretation is a doubtful one, and for a variety of reasons. Eduard Schweizer writes,

> "...first, Jesus paid close attention to earthly needs and their alleviation; second, the next petition, and probably the one following, refer unambiguously to this world, where men wrong each other and must find again the path of reconciliation; and third, if the plea were eschatological the word 'our' would be out of place. Furthermore, wine and fat meat—not bread— are characteristic of the eschatological banquet."[5]

Jesus is referring to material survival, here and now. This seems to be confirmed in the discourse on dealing with scarcity which follows (Mt. 6:25-34; Lk. 12:22-31).

Those listening to Jesus are advised that the rational course is to avoid anxiety about consumption requirements. Arguments for adopting this course include: life means more than food and clothes (Mt. 6:25); men are worth more than birds, yet God cares for these lesser creatures (Mt. 6:26); and, worry about the duration of one's life avails nothing (Mt. 6:27). Jesus goes on to compare the appearance of the flowers of the field with that of Solomon; and he declares the King's robes inferior. The inference is that the Solution by Wisdom (so closely associated with Solomon) is no match for the one which Jesus is proposing.

This particular section of the Sermon then moves to its climax with a statement of the strategy to be adopted for solving the economic problem. Scarcity is dealt with by seeking the kingdom and living in terms of that realm. Jesus concludes: "Therefore do not be anxious saying, 'What shall we eat?' or 'What shall we drink?' or 'What shall we wear?' For the Gentiles seek all these things; and your heavenly Father knows that you need them all. But seek first his kingdom and his righteousness, and all these things shall be yours as well. Therefore do not be anxious about tomorrow, for tomorrow will be anxious for itself. Let the day's own trouble be sufficient for the day." (Mt. 6:31-34; R.S.V. See also, Lk. 12:29-31).

The Solution by Seeking the Kingdom, it is clear, involves: trust in the Father; a willingness to recognise personal dependence; and low valua-

---

[4] See, e.g., R. E. Brown, op.cit., pp. 194-9.
[5] E. Schweizer, op.cit., p. 154. See also, I. H. Marshall, op.cit., pp. 458-60; and, Aelred Baker, "What Sort of Bread did Jesus want us to Pray For?", *New Blackfriars*, 54 (1973), pp. 125-9.

tion, in the present, of possible future personal utilities. Also, it involves rejection of one's own material welfare as the focal point of activity. Satisfaction of needs, in that regard, comes as a by-product. This feature has been noted by Howard Marshall who writes that there is, "the positive command to the disciples that instead of seeking after material things they are to seek for the kingdom of God; if they do this (*parataxis*, equivalent to a condition), the material things will be given to them in addition."[6] It is notable too that the term "seek" is used, rather than "find". This suggests that there must be a willingness to live with uncertainty and to take risks, just as Abraham and Moses were obliged to do in the course of their journeys.

It might be objected that the foregoing is not intended as anything other than a prescription for behaviour appropriate for a world which is soon to end. However, as William Davies points out: "What we find in the Sermon on the Mount is not an ethic for those who expect the speedy end of the world but for those who have experienced the end of this world and the coming of the Kingdom of God."[7] In this regard, it is relevant to observe that the assertion which is at the core of this Solution, namely, the care of the Father for each individual, is repeated elsewhere by Matthew in contexts which do not have any discernible reference to an end of the world (see, e.g. Mt. 7:7-11; 10:29-31; 18:19-20).

Another line of objection to Jesus' Solution as a prescription for dealing with economic reality is its omission of any explicit reference to the role that work may play in the lives of his followers. However, such an objection overlooks the fact that Jesus was a Jew preaching to other Jews dwelling in the Land. Jesus and his audience took for granted that they had been formed in the image of God as workers (see, Chapter One). Seeking, or setting one's heart on, the Father's kingdom did not imply the abandonment of usual productive activities. In fact, the new Solution implied a fresh perspective on work which evoked its pre-Fall significance as expounded in *Genesis*. That perspective is portrayed in the manner in

---

[6] I. H. Marshall, op.cit., p. 530. Here, Marshall is referring to Luke 12:31 which is the verse corresponding to Matthew 6:33. The key role of Mt. 6:33 has been recognised by Martin Hengel. He writes that, "the demand in the Sermon on the Mount (Matt. 6:33) is fundamental to any understanding of his (Jesus') attitude to all earthly goods." M. Hengel, *Property and Riches in the Early Church* (London: S. C. M., 1974), p. 24. Duncan Derrett comments: "Those who make a struggle for the Kingdom their principal concern will not be devoid of social and economic ingenuity. Their judgement will not be vitiated by distractions such as mere concern for their personal alimentation and apparel". J. D. M. Derrett, "Birds of the Air and Lilies of the Field", *Downside Review*, No. 360 (July 1987), p. 190.

[7] W. D. Davies, *The Setting of the Sermon on the Mount* (Cambridge: Cambridge University Press, 1966), p. 219.

which Jesus lived his public life, and in the content of some of his teaching by means of parables.[8] Jesus took on an extremely demanding work-schedule when "his time" came. The schedule, it must be admitted, allowed for tablefellowship, the cementing of friendships, and enjoyment of the festivals provided for in the Law. Jesus was not a self-lacerating workaholic. Nevertheless, his tasks involved very considerable psychic and physical costs.

WORKING FOR THE FATHER

The gospel records of his adult life, records which we must use even if we admit that the evangelists were writing 'theologies' not biographies, make it plain that Jesus is a man wrestling with a particularly difficult job specification, but one he is determined to carry through. His job involves risk-taking and a good deal of innovatory activity. In addition, there is a high degree of work-tension, since, as Markus Barth points out, "Jesus Christ is not given a detailed job description. Rather he is trusted to act out freely what pleases the Father."[9]

Any serious analysis of Jesus as a worker, it should be emphasised, is entirely vitiated by a focus on "Jesus the Carpenter." Alan Richardson, for example, observes that, "the New Testament writers do not seem to have been aware of any special significance attaching to Christ's fulfilment as techton (artisan, carpenter) of the ordinance of work."[10] Of course, the designation of Christ as "a carpenter" is important in both theological and sociological terms. It indicates, amongst other things, that Jesus did not own a part of the Land, and that he was not amongst the poorest of the poor (the agricultural day-labourers). However, this detail is of marginal relevance only for the evangelists' treatments of Jesus as a worker.

Much of the drama of the gospels turns around the efforts of Jesus to get his work done despite repeated frustrations from a variety of quarters. Jesus has been given a job specification by his Father. He is determined to act in terms of it. Friends, family, disciples, and the Establishment continually seek to weaken his resolve in this respect, but he holds to the general drift of the specification.

---

[8] C.f., John Paul II, *Laborem Exercens: On Human Work* (Sydney: St. Paul Publishers, 1981, p. 102. This Encyclical emphasises here, "the great though discreet gospel of work that we find in the life and parables of Christ, in what Jesus 'did and taught' ".

[9] M. Barth, *The Anchor Bible: Ephesians* (N.Y.: Doubleday, 1974), p. 109.

[10] A. Richardson, *The Biblical Doctrine of Work* (London: S.C.M., 1958), p. 47. C.f., the very careful treatment of the "carpenter" theme in John Paul II, op.cit., pp. 99, 101. Consult also, G. Vermes, op.cit., pp. 21-2.

Apart from some few treasured interludes when he is able to converse with his Father, or to enjoy in company the corn and the wine and the oil which his Father bestows, Jesus is ''on the road''. In addition, there is the continuous problem of his balancing the various facets of his task. Fundamentally, his work is to inform the Jewish people about the real character of the Father, and to enable them to make the appropriate response to the knowledge gained. This work requires him to teach, heal, feed, and die in a blaze of publicity. Dying, it must be emphasised is part of the work-plan, as Jesus explains (see, e.g., Jn. 3:13-15; 8:28-29). Each of the gospel writers is quite clear on this point. As J. Duncan M. Derrett writes:

> "The tradition was that Jesus gave up the spirit, and the implication of the whole story, as all four gospels confirm, was that Jesus died prematurely, i.e., much sooner than any skilled person would have expected, indeed so much sooner that suspicions were aroused that all was not above board. The implication with which all four evangelists leave us is that Jesus determined when to die, master of the situation to the last."[11]

Getting the right balance between the work of teaching and the work of dying is a major problem for Jesus in the *Gospel according to John.* From the very opening of his public life, the Jewish authorities are given good grounds for beginning to suspect that Jesus is a prime national security risk. John the Baptist draws public attention to Jesus at Bethany, just near Jerusalem (Jn. 1:29-34). Mary, Jesus' mother, follows suit at Cana in Galilee. Despite Jesus' demur concerning his ''hour'', Mary is instrumental in having Jesus perform a miracle to overcome a domestic scarcity problem for his hosts at a wedding feast (Jn. 2:1-12). Then, Jesus goes to Jerusalem itself, and ''devoured by zeal for his Father's house'', he whips the traders from the Temple (Jn. 2:13-17).

It is not long then, before Jesus becomes a man on the run, whose work is a dangerous game. Jesus learns that the activities of his disciples have come to the attention of the influential Pharisee party, so he finds it politic to leave Judaea and return to Galilee for a time (Jn. 4:1-3). Here, as Rudolf Schnackenburg remarks, ''Jesus is trying to avoid for the present an open conflict with the leading circles of Judaism, in keeping with his Father's will.''[12] Later, back in Jerusalem, Jesus' work-ethic brings him into conflict with the authorities. He heals on the Sabbath day, and he declares: ''My Father goes on working, and so do I.'' (Jn. 5:17). This declaration itself, more than the breaking of the Sabbath, upsets the

---

[11] J. D. M. Derrett, *Jesus's Audience* (London: Darton, Longman and Todd, 1973), p. 196.
[12] R. Schnackenburg, *The Gospel According to St. John,* Vol. I (London: Burns and Oates, 1968), p. 422.

Establishment, since, "the assumption of a uniform activity common to Jesus and to God could only mean that Jesus was equal to God."[13]

The threat of death is ever present as Jesus continues to teach (Jn. 7:1,30; 8:20, 58-59; 10:31-33), but matters come to a head when at Bethany, Jesus raises Lazarus from the dead. The authorities have been patient and cautious to this stage. However, they believe that now they must act to stop Jesus working. The Sanhedrin reasons: "If we let him go on in this way everybody will believe in him, and the Romans will come and destroy the Holy Place and our nation." (Jn. 1:48).[14] From this point on, Jesus' fate is sealed. For a time, he keeps himself hidden and manages to continue teaching, but the work of dying in accord with the will of his Father is delayed only until the Passover.

The problems of Jesus in his work are portrayed in somewhat different fashion in the *Gospel according to Mark*. There is no doubt, however, that Jesus is a man trying to respond to intense work pressure. As Gerard Sloyan comments: "If the Master relaxes, one does not learn it from Mark. To read this Gospel at a single sitting is to feel hemmed in by crowds, wearied by their demands, besieged by the attacks of demons."[15]

Many instances are illustrative of this. For example, at one point, the crowds prevent Jesus from snatching the rare opportunity of participating in a family meal (Mk. 3:20-21). At another point, he is so exhausted that he sleeps on in a small boat which is about to be sunk in a violent storm (Mk. 4:37-38). Not only Jesus, but his apostles find Jesus' kind of work extraordinarily demanding (Mk. 6:30-31).

There are links in Mark with the work-tension which, as we have seen, is central to the Gospel of John. To avoid dying before other aspects of his work are attended to, Jesus takes steps to keep his true identity hidden for a time. In Mark, in particular, it is the "devils" or "unclean spirits" who continually try to subvert Jesus' work by premature public exposure of who he really is (Mk. 1:25, 34; 3:11-12). Jesus silences these. Later, when the apostles have come to learn the truth, they too are told to keep silent (Mk. 8:27-30). It is apparent that Jesus' worry here is with the Jewish authorities, since he has no hesitation in having his exploits broadcast in a region such as the Decapolis (Mk. 5:19-20).

Another type of work-tension which is prominent in Mark's gospel is that between healing and teaching. This tension is established at a very

---

[13] C. K. Barrett, *The Gospel According to St. John*, (2nd ed.; London: S.P.C.K., 1978), p. 256.

[14] This reasoning is understandable in the contemporary context. See, ibid., p. 406, and, J. D. M. Derrett, *Law in the New Testament* (London: Darton, Longman and Todd, 1970), pp. 418-20.

[15] G. S. Sloyan, *The Gospel of Saint Mark* (Collegeville, Minn.: Liturgical Press, 1960), p. 7.

early stage in the narrative. In the first chapter of the Gospel, Jesus begins teaching in the synagogue at Capernaum. There, an unclean spirit endeavours to reveal that he is "the Holy One of God", but Jesus drives out this spirit, thus curing the man it was afflicting. Word of this spreads rapidly, and Jesus is soon engaged full-time in healing. Then, in the small hours of the morning, Jesus slips away to pray, and is tracked down by his disciples. At this, Jesus declares: "Let us go elsewhere, to the neighbouring country towns, so that I can preach there too, because that is why I came." (Mk. 1:38).

Mark continues to refer to this tension (see, e.g., Mk. 2:1-4; 5:42-43; 7:36; 8:26). However, it takes on even greater proportions in the *Gospel of Matthew*, since for this evangelist the healing aspect of Jesus' work is especially important. "The Matthaean Jesus", as Davies has remarked, "is never merely a teacher."[16] Yet, even Matthew leaves the reader with the strong impression that before he commits himself to the work of dying, Jesus is a dedicated teacher whose work is constantly being interrupted by demands placed on him by virtue of his other concerns and abilities.

Service of others through hard work is a keynote of Matthew's gospel. Thus, in the sequence which immediately precedes the Sermon on the Mount (Mt. 4:18-25), when Jesus calls Peter, Andrew, James and John to abandon their nets and their boats, they are at once plunged into the demands of following him as assistants in a round of teaching and healing in Galilee. They do not give up their normal productive activities to contemplate the lilies of the field.

After the Sermon on the Mount, Jesus resumes healing immediately (Mt. 8:1-17). The pressure soon becomes overwhelming in terms of his overall work-plan and, in sheer physical terms. He decides to escape for a while across the Lake, and he comments: "Foxes have holes and the birds of the air have nests, but the Son of Man has nowhere to lay his head." (Mt. 8:20). Even more to the point, he advises one of his disciples: "Follow me, and leave the dead to bury their dead." (Mt. 8:22). Shortly after, as in the Gospel of Mark, Jesus sleeps in a boat about to sink in a raging storm (Mt. 8:23-25).

Eventually, the opportunity cost of healing, in terms of his mission as a teacher, reaches such a height that Jesus decides to assign much of what might otherwise be demanded of him to the apostles (Mt. 9:36-10:8). He gives the apostles the power to heal, and instructs them as to how they should begin to undertake this type of work. Then, he turns to endeavour to concentrate on the work for which he is uniquely fitted: "When Jesus

---

[16] W. D. Davies, op.cit., p. 28. See also, E. Schweizer, op.cit., p. 381.

had finished instructing his twelve disciples he moved on from there to teach and preach in their towns." (Mt. 11:1).

As this Gospel continues, however, Jesus does not give up healing entirely at this particular point. Admittedly, a deal of the subsequent healing occurs in a teaching context (Mt. 12:9-14; 12:22-37; 17:14-20), but it is also undertaken as a response to "great faith" (Mt. 15:21-28) and out of pity (Mt. 20:29-43). It is also out of pity that twice Jesus confronts scarcity directly by expanding meagre supplies of food to more than satisfy the demands of thousands (Mt. 14:13-21; 15:32-39). Even on his way to Jerusalem for what Jesus sees as the completion of the job-plan given by his Father (death and resurrection), he is willing to turn aside to heal the two blind men of Jericho who implore his services (Mt. 20:29-34).

The last mention of Jesus' healing, in Matthew, occurs when Jesus enters the Temple. He cures those who come to him there (Mt. 21:14). Thereafter he goes on teaching, and at considerable length; but once he is arrested, the focus is on the work of dying. Before the Sanhedrin, before Pilate, and on the Cross, there is little attempt to communicate. Once Jesus is dead, buried and risen, however, the work of teaching returns. In the last verses of this Gospel, the apostles are told to baptise and teach with the assurance that Jesus is with them in this work to the end of time (Mt. 28:19-20).

Paul and Work

The strong work-ethic that emerges from the gospel accounts of the last years of Jesus' life is even more explicit in the letters of Saint Paul. There are between ten and fourteen of these letters, and they were addressed to a variety of the urban Christian communities founded in the two or three decades after Jesus' execution. The earliest of the letters may date from A.D.49. The last letter was probably written between A.D.58 and A.D.62. Paul's readers represented a substantial cross-section of the city dwellers of commercially significant Mediterranean centres. Some were Jews, others were Pagans, and a proportion of them were well-to-do citizens. Prisca and Aquila, for example, had extensive commercial interests. Crispus was the head of the synagogue in Corinth. Erastus was the treasurer of the same City. In the opinion of Martin Hengel: "The majority of early Christians will have belonged to the 'middle class' of antiquity from which the 'godfearers' of the Jewish mission were recruited."[17]

---

[17] M. Hengel, *Property and Riches in the Early Church* (London: S.C.M., 1974), pp. 36-8. Consult also, E. A. Judge, *The Social Pattern of Christian Groups in the First Century* (London: Tyndale Press, 1960).

"In the ancient world", observes Eduard Lohse, "the view was widespread that by asceticism and fasting man served the deity, came closer to him, or could prepare himself to receive a divine revelation."[18] Paul has no time at all for this view. Paul, it is clear, is no advocate of an individual's embracing poverty for its own sake. When he asks the Corinthians for money to help the needy in Jerusalem, for example, he stresses that the givers should not impoverish themselves. (2 Co.8:12-13). Again, writing to the Philippians, he states that, as for himself, he is just as ready to be rich as poor. He can cope with either circumstance (Ph.4:10-13). Paul, "is not devoted to hardship for its own sake. Unlike the Cynic, he does not go out of his way to get along on as little as possible."[19]

Paul is absolutely opposed to the idea of the right to a share in the output of the community for the voluntarily unemployed. To the Thessalonians, he writes:

> "In the name of the Lord Jesus Christ, we urge you, brothers, to keep away from any of the brothers who refuses to work or to live according to the tradition we passed on to you. We gave you a rule when we were with you: not to let anyone have any food if he refused to do any work." (2 Th. 3:6, 10).

Later, Paul instructs the Ephesians: "Anyone who was a thief must stop stealing; he should try to find some useful manual work instead, and be able to do some good by helping others that are in need." (Ep. 4:28).

The subject of work looms large in Paul's epistles, partly because it represented a major pastoral problem for him. There were many in his newly formed church communities who were influenced by the Greek idea that manual labour was degrading for free men. Many would have agreed with the poet Homer (*Iliad*, 10, 71) that work is, "the most oppressive misfortune that Zeus imposes upon men from their very birth." This idea was entirely unacceptable to Paul both as a Jew and as a Christian. Markus Barth writes: "It can easily be explained why Paul laid emphasis on manual labour. Most rabbis of his as well as of later times made their living in some civic profession, preferably as artisans... But not only a rabbinical and Pharisaical tradition is reflected in the command to 'work'. According to Mark 3:1-6 Jesus himself healed in a synagogue a man's 'withered hand', and thereby 'saved life' (Mark 3:4) and restored a man's ability to earn his livelihood."[20]

---

[18] E. Lohse, *Colossians and Philemon* (Philadelphia: Fortress, 1971), p. 115.

[19] F. W. Beare, *A Commentary on the Epistle to the Philippians*, (London: Black, 1969), p. 152.

[20] M. Barth, op.cit., p. 516. C.f., Ernest Best, *A Commentary on the First and Second Epistles to the Thessalonians* (London: Black, 1972), pp. 103-4. Concerning this episode, see also, J. Duncan, M. Derrett, *The Making of Mark*, Vol. I (Shipston: Drinkwater, 1985), pp. 77-82.

Work was also a pastoral problem, in that it seemed to have little point to some Christians. The religion they had adopted had been launched at a time when apocalyptic expectation was widespread and highly charged. Their new faith did not deny the validity of such expectation, in that it affirmed the future parousia of the risen Christ. It could be argued that if that parousia was imminent and the End to come soon, then toil was purposeless. Better to concentrate on preparing one self and others for the End rather than bother to continue the age-old battle with scarcity. Soon, scarcity would be vanquished by the direct action of God himself. The powers and principalities of this world who continued to hide the means of life from men would be overthrown.

Right from his very first epistle, Paul sets out to combat anti-work sentiments among his new Christians. In the first place, he tells them that he has absolutely no idea when the End is to come: "You will not be expecting us to write anything to you, brothers, about 'times and seasons', since you know very well that the day of the Lord is going to come like a thief in the night." (1 Th. 5:1-2).[21] One obvious inference is that it is foolish to base one's behaviour in either the short or medium terms on the assumption that the Day when scarcity disappears is sure to fall within those limits. In the second place, he leads by example in that he allocates much of his own time and energy to the mundane business of earning a living. He asks the Thessalonians to recall that allocation: "Let me remind you, brothers, how hard we used to work, slaving night and day so as not to be a burden on any one of you while we were proclaiming God's Good News to you." (1 Th. 2:9).[22]

This latter passage indicates the extraordinarily heavy emphasis which Paul placed on self-sufficiency as a primary goal of economic activity at the micro level. A Christian, according to Paul, works so as not to impose himself as a drain on the output of others. However, there is more involved than this. He also works so as not to bring discredit on his faith-community in the eyes of those who are outside it. The sensibilities of non-Christians are not to be trampled upon. Paul writes, "we do urge you, brothers, to go on making even greater progress and to make a point of living quietly, attending to your own business and earning your living, just as we told you to, so that you are seen to be respectable by those outside the Church, and (or, though) you do not have to depend on them." (1 Th. 4:10-12). Beyond this, there is the consideration of being in a position to come to the aid of those in need (Ep. 4:28). Also, engage-

---

[21] C.f. 2 Th. 2:1f.
[22] C.f. 2 Th. 3:7-9, and 1 Co. 4-12.

ment in work decreases the likelihood that one will reduce the productivity of others (2 Th. 3:11-12).

Such was Paul's attachment to the aim of self-sufficiency that he attempted to live the "double life" of artisan and evangelist. Paul, it would seem, set out to prove a point, and he believed that it would clarify the content of his missionary message if he was able to differentiate himself from other types of travelling teachers who looked to their pupils for payment in return for instruction. However, with his customary candour he admits that this did not always prove feasible.

LIVING IN THE HOUSEHOLD

According to some commentators, there are dimensions to Paul's treatment of work which go beyond those considered thus far. There are strong linguistic grounds for such a view. As Karl Schelkle points out: "Under a single term he (Paul) includes both manual *labor* and Apostolic ministry. (1 Thess. 2:9, Rom. 16:12; 1 Cor. 15:58; 2 Cor. 10:15). The linguistic usage that can use the term labor both for manual toil and for ministry, probably invented by Paul, is continued in the Acts of the Apostles (20:35), as also in the Pastoral Epistles (1 Tim. 4:10; 5:17)... In the saying, 'Whatever you do, in word or work, do all in the name of the Lord Jesus' (Col. 3:17), the term *work* is used in a comprehensive sense. It includes, in a special way, the work of labor."[23] The inference is, that a deal of what Paul says about the significance of the apostolic ministry can be applied to the economic involvements of Christians.

Perhaps the most substantive feature of these further dimensions is Paul's use of the idea of work as service within a "household." In the household, as Paul conceives it, the head is God the Father, Yahweh. The administrator, or steward, entrusted with ensuring that the household runs according to the wishes of its head, is the Son, Jesus.[24] Further, in obedience to those wishes, the steward has purchased slaves from the households of other masters and attached them to that of the Father. These slaves are Paul and his fellow Christians. In their new circumstances, those who have been bought are expected to serve Jesus the steward as if they still had the status of slave.[25] Yet, in reality, that is no

---

[23] K. H. Schelkle, *Theology of the New Testament, Vol. 3* (Collegeville, Minn.: Liturgical Press, 1973), pp. 294-5.

[24] Consult, J. Reumann, "Jesus the Steward: an Over-looked Theme in Christology", in F. L. Cross (ed.), *Studia Evangelica*, Vol. V (Berlin: Akademie-Verlag, 1968), pp. 21-9.

[25] "The same Greek word (douleuo) is used for the idea of 'being a slave' and of 'service', because in the ancient world these ideas were often inseparable." Donald Guthrie, *Galatians* (London: Oliphants, 1977), p. 116.

longer their status. Each has been given the rights of a son and heir in the household. The question arises as to why they should continue as servants, given their sonship. The reasons include, love of the beneficent Father who willed their being purchased and, imitation of his Son who bought them by dying the death of a slave, i.e. crucifixion.[26]

Membership of this household, in Paul's estimation, is the ultimate social reality in the life of a Christian. Hence, any of his other social engagements are to be referred back to it for any assessment of their ultimate worth. Work is one such engagement, and so Paul urges that it be done, "for the sake of the Lord and not for the sake of men" (Ep. 6:7). Jesus the Steward is the final arbiter of the diligence with which an individual has responded to the Father's plan that man would be a worker. Further, it is by serving the Steward that the Father's intentions are met. As Paul writes in the Haustafeln (rules for the household) when he is counselling Christians who are slaves:

> "Slaves, be obedient to men who are called your masters in this world; not only when you are under their eye, as if you had only to please men, but wholeheartedly, out of respect for the Master. Whatever your work is, put your heart into it as if it were for the Lord and not for men, knowing that the Lord will repay you by making you his heirs. It is Christ the Lord that you are serving." (Col. 3:22-24).

Passages such as this seem to offer something new in terms of biblical thinking on work. Commenting on the above, Alan Richardson writes: "The sanction of the Christian ethic of work is not any natural law, such as the Stoic might recognise, nor even any divine ordinance which the Old Testament might enshrine, but the obedience which the Christian owes to his heavenly Master."[27] Each Christian then, should be a patient, toiling servant-slave. Paul emphasises this in his writings by frequently applying the term, "doulos" to himself (e.g. Rm. 1:1; Ph. 1:1; Ga. 1:10; 2 Co. 4:5).[28] This is not to say, however, that the Christian in work must be a passive menial. To the contrary, he should exercise such powers of administrative ability and entreprneurial flair as have been given him. Hence, Paul also frequently proclaims himself a steward, charged with the responsibilities of organisation and innovation.[29]

---

[26] The reasoning here is illuminated by reference to Roman family law. Consult, R. G. Tanner, "Jesus and the Fatherhood of God", *Colloquium*, 3 (1968), pp. 201-10.

[27] Alan Richardson, *The Biblical Doctrine of Work* (London: S.C.M., 1958), pp. 42-3.

[28] David Stanley finds that *doulos* is Paul's "favourite title for himself". See, D. M. Stanley, "The Theme of the Servant of Yahweh in Primitive Christian Soteriology and its Transposition by St. Paul", *Catholic Biblical Quarterly*, 16 (1954), pp. 417-8.

[29] Consult, J. Reumann, "Oikonomia—Terms in Paul in Comparison with Lucan *Heilsgeschichte*", *New Testament Studies*, 13 (1966-67), pp. 147-67. In the ancient world

In conclusion, it must be remarked that while Paul's assessments of the meaning of work and its relationship to the problem of scarcity are quite compatible with those of Jesus, the apostle does not situate his analysis within the context of "the kingdom". Probably, this is due to the strong contrasts in the social setting of Paul's preaching as compared with that of Jesus. It may have been both compromising and dangerous for Paul to have used "the kingdom" as a term in his letters. As Davies has observed,

> "When Paul discovered that the term 'Kingdom of God' had disturbing political implications, he was led to drop it from his vocabulary."[30]

Focus on the household was an apt substitute, since in Paul's era the household meant an extended community of consumers and producers sharing a common fate. However, "the household" lacked the inherent dynamic of "the kingdom". The latter could be portrayed as "coming", whereas the former could not. Hence, Paul's economic thought has a static quality which does not do justice to the dynamism suggested in Jesus' terminology.

WORK AND THE PARABLES

"That the Kingdom of Heaven is mixed with this world, inextricably until the end of the age," writes Derrett, "is after all the message of numerous parables."[31] Part of that "mixture" comprises the conduct and consequences of everyday work, so it is not surprising that the parables refer to men engaged in a wide range of employments. Whether or not the parables offer a doctrine of work, however, is open to debate, since much depends on how the character of parable is to be interpreted.[32] On the other hand, it is clear that the parables offer abundant *materials* for such a doctrine.

It can be claimed that several of the parables display an understanding of work which is closely allied to that of Saint Paul. Such parables

---

there was no contradiction between being a slave and the occupancy of high offices. On this, see, e.g. A. Richardson, op.cit., p. 42; and E. Barker, *From Alexander to Constantine* (Oxford: Clarendon, 1956), p. 405.

[30] W. D. Davies, "The Relevance of the Moral Teaching of the Early Church", in, E. Earle Ellis and Max Wilcox (eds.), *Neotestamentica et Semitica* (Edinburgh: Clark, 1969), p. 39.

[31] J. D. M. Derrett, *Law in the New Testament* (London: Darton, Longman and Todd, 1970), p. 92.

[32] On the character of parable, consult, C. H. Dodd, *The Parables of the Kingdom* (London: Collins, 1971), Ch. 1. See also, Joachim Jeremias, *The Parables of Jesus* (London: S.C.M., 1971), Chs. 1 and 2; and, Eta Linnemann, *Parables of Jesus* (London: S.P.C.K., 1975), Part 1.

include: the Parable of Faithful Stewardship (Lk. 16:10-13); the Parable of Responsibility (Mt. 25:14-30; c.f. Lk. 19:11-27); and, the Parable of the Unprofitable Servant (Lk. 17:7-10). Reflecting on these, Kenneth Russell has concluded that, "it is clear that man's service to God is not just vaguely similar to the slave's service to a master. Man truly stands as a slave in complete and utter dependence on God. His life and every action should be the expression of his essential *ebed*hood."[33]

If there is a doctrine of work in the parables, then it is rather more wide-ranging than that of the Pauline epistles. Paul, as we have seen, is anxious that everyone, "should stay as he was before God at the time of his call." (1 Co. 7:24). Rather like the Socratic philosophers, Paul implies a static economy with unchanging work-patterns as an ideal. He seems entirely innocent of the idea of economic development. This is not the case with some of the parables. These treat work as an exercise in enterprise, risk-taking, and entrepreuneurship—aspects of work which are at the core of the development process.

In the Parable of Responsibility (or, the Talents) (Mt. 25:14-30) the servant (or slave) of God is no mere passive menial.[34] Instead, he is obliged to be innovative. This story relates how a timorous servant, in contrast with his more enterprising counterparts, fails to realise either profit or interest on the capital entrusted to him. He is condemned by the master, while the two other servants, who have shown some imagination and daring, are rewarded. Eduard Schweizer comments:

> "Two of the servants take a risk, which of course could entail the loss of everything entrusted to them, because they know what their lord has given them must be actively at work, must live, must effect something new... The parable is aimed at those devoted to their own personal security, devoted to the vindication of their own righteousness, rather than being devoted to God, which means being devoted to other people, taking active (and risky) steps to help them."[35]

Astute commercial behaviour is commended also in the extraordinarily opaque parable which opens the sixteenth chapter of Luke's gospel. The steward of this story is labelled variously by modern commentators as being "unjust", "dishonest", "crafty", or "prudent". Much doubt surrounds the significance of the master's praising the strategy of the business agent concerned (Lk. 16:8). From the standpoint of a doctrine of work, however, it is notable that some modern scholars find that this

---

[33] K. C. Russell, "Slavery as Reality and Metaphor in the Non-Pauline New Testament Books", *Revue de l'Université d'Ottawa*, 42 (1972), p. 455.

[34] Derrett (ibid., pp. 18-9) contends that here we are dealing with servants who are not slaves. A slave could not have been permitted such a free hand with capital.

[35] E. Schweizer, op.cit., p. 471-2.

parable is about the right use of wealth, and that the astute steward is meant to be a model in this regard.[36]

These examples indicate the *potential* of the parables for an understanding of what Jesus meant to convey on the subject of work. His own life, and his instructions to his immediate disciples, recommend devoted response to the needs of others as the keynote. That response, as his Solution with respect to Scarcity indicates, is not to be governed by calculations about the fulfilment of the worker's own consumption requirements. Coverage of these latter can be safely assigned to the Father.[37] The parables do not contest this basic stance. Rather, a number of them suggest that Jesus was prepared to incorporate within his schema a much wider range of human activities than his own work-plan and that appropriate for his most immediate companions could admit, given the exigencies of place, talent, and time.

---

[36] For a comprehensive survey of opinion, consult I.H. Marshall, op.cit., pp. 614-22. Especially interesting is the analysis by J. D. M. Derrett, ibid., pp. 48-77.

[37] In terms of modern Western culture, something of what Jesus meant is illustrated by the "professional ideal", e.g., the lifestyle of a devoted general practitioner of medicine.

CHAPTER SIX

DISCIPLESHIP, DISINVESTMENT AND DEPENDENCE

> "None of you can be my disciple unless he gives up all his possessions."
>
> *Gospel of Luke* 14:33.

Some contributors to the literature of the *New Testament* appear to require the follower of Jesus to eschew economic self-sufficiency, and to undertake disinvestment as a quite deliberate policy. The Christian, according to these authors, should command no capital, but rather, must seek to become dependent on the investments of others in order to survive in the face of the problem of scarcity of resources which was engendered by the Fall. Any Christian worth the name embraces material poverty. The Epistle of James and sections of the Gospel of Luke illustrate such tendencies.

THE EPISTLE OF JAMES

In this document, Christianity is associated with the type of idealization of the poor which had begun to make its mark in Jewish thought during the era of the declining political autonomy of Israel. Concerning the background to *James*, Martin Dibelius writes:

> "In Israel, as in every healthy human society, poverty was originally considered a disadvantage, not something good. Only when Israel no longer possessed her national strength did the idea win acceptance that the poor man was close to God in a special way."[1]

This idea provides a major theme of the epistle. Such is the emphasis, in fact, that those who are not poor are given little chance for any salutary relationship with God.

Opinion is divided, but *James* is probably a very early Christian composition. It could even be pre-Pauline. Eugene Maly, for example, states:

> "There are many indications that the epistle of James is one of the earliest writings of the New Testament. The references to Christ are few and of a simple nature suggesting a primitive period when a detailed doctrine on

---

[1] M. Dibelius, *A Commentary on the Epistle of James* (11th ed., revised by Heinrich Greeven; Philadelphia: Fortress, 1976), p. 39.

Christ had not yet been formulated... we can suppose that the letter was written about the middle of the first century.''[2]

There is a long tradition ascribing the authorship to a "James" who was a prominent figure in the Christian community in Jerusalem.[3] This tradition has some merit, especially in that the sentiments of the epistle concerning economic activity are very much in accord with what can be learned from the *Acts of the Apostles* about the economic behaviour of the Jerusalem Christians. These indulged in disinvestment on a considerable scale.[4] The writer of *James* gives the strongest of impressions that this is the only wise course for a Christian with assets.

From the outset of this short letter, the author contrasts the excellence of poverty with the baseness of riches. The poor man is to be proud of his status, whereas the one who is rich can look forward only to his own humiliation (1:9-10). The ephemeral nature of accumulated wealth is emphasised, as is the brevity of the span of time over which it can be commanded by any one person. "His business goes on", is the comment, "he himself perishes." (1:11). There is no suggestion here that the successful capitalist might be consoled by the thought that he has left his heirs in a good position to carry on his work and his name. Such a suggestion could have come naturally from a Jewish writer of some earlier era.

In his life-time, the man who seeks wealth by commercial endeavour condemns himself to a precarious existence. Uncertainty and failure of expectations, it is observed, are part and parcel of the world of trade (4:13-14). At the end of his life he can expect misery and "a burning fire" (5:1-4). The poor man, it is allowed, can expect some suffering during his earthly existence. But, this suffering has a rationale in that it is a "test" from which he can derive "patience", and hence, a degree of personal development which may not have been attained otherwise (1:2-4). As for earthly happiness, this will be enjoyed by, "the man who looks steadily at the perfect law of freedom and makes that his habit." (1:25).[5] At the end, the poor man can expect to inherit the kingdom of

[2] E. H. Maly, *The Epistles of Saints James, Jude, Peter* (Collegeville, Minn.: Liturgical Press, 1960), p. 5. c.f., J. A. T. Robinson, *Redating the New Testament* (London: S.C.M., 1976). For argument in favour of a much later dating see, M. Dibelius, *A Commentary on the Epistle of James*, pp. 44-5.

[3] On the figure "James", see Jacob Jervell, *Luke and the People of God* (Minneapolis: Augsburg, 1979), pp. 185-207.

[4] c.f. M. Hengel, *Property and Riches in the Early Church*, (London: S.C.M., 1974), pp. 31-4; and, I. Howard Marshall, *Luke: Historian and Theologian* (Exeter: Paternoster, 1979), p. 208. Consult also, Ernst Haenchen, *The Acts of the Apostles, a Commentary* (Oxford: Blackwell, 1971), pp. 230-241.

[5] In the background of this reasoning there stands the long tradition of Jewish reflection on the deprivations of the just.

God. The poor have been especially chosen as the inheritors of that realm
(2:5).[6]

The foregoing set of statements constitute the narrowest treatment of
religion in relation to economic activity which is encountered in the New
Testament. Martin Dibelius remarks that what is set forth here is a
"conventicle-ethic", and he continues:

> "This conventicular self-limitation differed, not to its advantage, from the
> inner freedom with which Jesus proclaimed repentance and forgiveness,
> from the missionary zeal of Paul, and from the universal tendencies of early
> Catholicism... our author's disposition is in fact to abandon the rich people
> to their destruction rather than to give them a welcome invitation to the
> Christian community, for their entrance into the community might corrupt
> its attitude of hostility toward the world and its pride amidst poverty."[7]

Some echoes of such a disposition, it might be contended, linger on in
the writings of Luke.

LUKE, JAMES AND PAUL

The gospel according to Luke is probably a later work than *James*. There
is a substantial measure of agreement among biblical scholars for setting
its date of composition as somewhere between AD.60 and AD.80. It is
anything but "primitive", being a well organised exposition of the life
and work of Jesus of Nazareth. In broad terms, the sequence which Luke
adopts for his exposition is, as follows: preface (1:1-14); the birth and
private life of Jesus (1:5-2:52); prelude to Jesus' public ministry (3:1-4.
13); the Galilean ministry (4:14-9:50); the journey to Jerusalem (9:51-
19:10); the Jerusalem ministry (19:11-21:38); the last supper, trial,
execution, and resurrection of Jesus (22:1-24:53).

In writing this work, the author drew on the Gospel of Mark, plus
other material relating to Jesus. He may also have been acquainted with
the Gospel of Matthew, but the priority of Matthew is a much contested
issue in modern research, and it is inappropriate to put too much stress
on this as a source, at present. Tradition has it that the author had been,
born to Greek parents at Antioch in Syria; educated in classical literature
and medicine; converted to Christianity as a young man; and, associated
with Paul on some of the latter's missionary journeys.[8] It is widely
accepted that he also composed the *Acts of the Apostles.*

---

[6] J. L. Houlden comments: "Some of this doctrine (especially ii, 5) is close to being
inverted snobbery at its simplest—an outburst of 'have nots' against the 'haves'." *Ethics
and the New Testament* (London and Oxford: Mowbrays, 1973), p. 89.

[7] M. Dibelius, *A Commentary on the Epistle of James*, p. 49.

[8] See, e.g. Carroll Stuhlmueller, *The Gospel of Saint Luke* (Collegeville, Minn.:
Liturgical Press, 1964), pp. 3-5. Each aspect of this tradition has been seriously questioned in modern scholarly debate.

Despite the tradition of the existence of close ties between Luke and Paul, it must be recognised that there are significant differences of emphasis in their thought. As Howard Marshall admits: ''There is no disputing that the theologies of Paul and of Luke are two different entities.''[9] Further, the economics of Luke is not the same as Paul's. The two writers differ markedly, for example, in their treatments of poverty, riches, and possessions. On these subjects, the author of the Gospel has often been thought to display a leaning towards the doctrines associated with the early, heretical Christian sect known as "the Ebionites". The same leaning is even more evident in the epistle of James.[10] Yet, it is impossible to detect any trace of such an affiliation in Paul who puts no great store on systematic voluntary restriction of consumption, or an abandonment of personal capital.

ASCETICISM AND POVERTY

In the early chapters of Luke, which are devoted to John the Baptist and the young Jesus, there is considerable attention given asceticism. John, so his mother is told, "must drink no wine, no strong drink."(1:15). As a young man, he lives out in the wilderness (1:80). Again, Anna the prophetess (who hails the child Jesus when he is presented to Yahweh in the Temple) is a woman who has devoted herself to decades of prayer and fasting (2:36-7). Jesus himself, before the commencement of his public ministry, fasts in the wilderness for forty days (4:1-3).

Poverty, in these early chapters, is portrayed as a circumstance which can be associated with the special care and favour of God. For example, in her "Magnificat", Mary the mother of Jesus states: "The hungry he (Yahweh) has filled with good things, the rich sent empty away."(1:53). The birth of Jesus takes place in conditions of physical difficulty where normal minima are absent (2:6-7). When that birth is announced by the angel of the Lord, the proclamation is made to, "shepherds who lived in the fields."(2:8). These were members of a very low economic stratum of Palestinian society. Again, when Jesus' parents make the offering required by law for the ritual cleansing of the mother—two doves or pigeons (2:24)—they take advantage of a concession which the law allowed the poor. Normally, a lamb and a pigeon were to be sacrificed.[11]

---

[9] I. H. Marshall, *Luke: Historian and Theologian*, p. 220.

[10] On Luke, James, and the Ebionite conception of poverty, see, R. Schnackenburg, *The Moral Teaching of the New Testament* (London: Burns and Oates, 1975), p. 127, 363. But, see also, I. H. Marshall, *Luke: Historian and Theologian*, p. 142.

[11] Consult, I. Howard Marshall, *The Gospel of Luke* (Exeter: Paternoster, 1978), pp. 117-8.

With Jesus' Galilean ministry, the stress on ascetical behaviour is consciously relegated to a minor place in favour of emphasis on consumption patterns appropriate to table companionship. The adoption of such patterns by Jesus and his followers is said to puzzle some contemporaries, who observe: "John's disciples are always fasting and saying prayers, and the disciples of the Pharisees too, but yours go on eating and drinking."(5:33). Later, Jesus himself states: "For John the Baptist comes, not eating bread, not drinking wine, and you say, 'He is possessed'. The Son of Man comes, eating and drinking, and you say, 'Look, a glutton and a drunkard, a friend of tax collectors and sinners.'" (7:33-4). From this it would appear that Jesus was not an ascetic, and was fond of festive gatherings.[12] The rationale of his approach to consumption behaviour is given by Edward Schillebeeckx, as follows:

> "Whereas John's call to conversion was essentially bound up with ascetic, penitential practices, the call of Jesus seems to have a fundamental connection with being a table-companion, eating and drinking together with Jesus, an activity in which Jesus' disciples could legitimately feel that the 'latter-day', that is, crucial and definitive, exercise of God's mercy was already present. To believe in Jesus is to put one's trust gladly in God; that is no occasion for fasting."[13]

Despite the foregoing shift, the theme of the special status of the poor is maintained. Jesus teaches:

> "How happy are you who are poor: yours is the kingdom of God. Happy you who are hungry now: you shall be satisfied. But alas for you who are rich: you are having your consolation now. Alas for you who have your fill now: you shall go hungry." (6:20-21, 24-25).[14]

During the journey to Jerusalem, this theme is expanded such that it would appear that anyone who is poor on earth can look forward to an eternal existence in union with God, while anyone who is affluent must expect damnation. This is the impression which might be gained from the story of the rich man and Lazarus (16:19-31), and from Jesus' declaration: "Yes, it is easier for a camel to pass through the eye of a needle than for a rich man to enter the kingdom of God."(18:25).

---

[12] c.f., M. Hengel, *Property and Riches in the Early Church*, p. 28.

[13] E. Schillebeeckx, *Jesus, an Experiment in Christology* (London: Collins, 1979), p. 204.

[14] There seems little doubt that "the poor" here are poor in economic terms. c.f., I. H. Marshall, *The Gospel of Luke*, pp. 249-50; and, R. Schnackenburg, *The Moral Teaching of the New Testament*, p. 128. Karl Schelkle comments: "In the discourse of Luke corresponding to Matthew's Sermon on the Mount, Jesus literally glorifies the poor and hungry, while he threatens the rich with his 'woe-betide-thee's' (Luke 6:20-26)." K. H. Schelkle, *Theology of the New Testament*, Vol III (Collegeville, Minn.: Liturgical Press, 1973), p. 309.

When the story and the declaration are considered in context, however, it is evident that Jesus is not predicting a simple reversal of fortunes
as between this world and the next. As Joachim Jeremias points out, the
story of the rich man and Lazarus is based on a folk-tale familiar to Jesus'
audience, so detail is not elaborated. Given that detail, it becomes
apparent that the lesson, ''is that impiety and lovelessness are punished,
and that piety and humility are rewarded.''[15] The rich man is condemned not for his wealth but rather, his lack of social concern. In the
case of the ''eye of a needle'' statement, it also emerges that the possession of wealth is not an absolute barrier to salvation. Howard Marshall
comments:

> ''Pressed by the disciples to explain such a drastic statement, which appears
> to rule out all hope of salvation for anybody, Jesus replies that, while it is
> certainly impossible from a human point of view, it is possible in terms of
> the power of God. The statement is not explained, but the point is that God
> can work the miracle of conversion in the hearts even of the rich.''[16]

DISCIPLESHIP AND DISINVESTMENT

Although the Jesus of Luke's gospel does not call his followers to
asceticism, nor, perhaps, to life-long poverty, he seems to require that
they give up ownership and control of any capital they may have
accumulated. Thus, near the beginning of the Galilean ministry, when
Simon, James and John are invited to go with Jesus, we are told: ''they
left everything and followed him.''(5:11). The same response to the
invitation is forthcoming from Levi the tax collector (5:28). Later, when
Jesus sends the twelve apostles out ''to proclaim the kingdom of God and
to heal'', he instructs them to go without capital in any shape or form.
Money, staff, haversack, bread, even a change of clothing—none of these
are to be taken (9:1-3). The obvious inference is that possession of
anything other than the clothes they stand up in is inimical to their mission. They must be utterly dependent.

The emphasis on decapitalisation is also well in evidence in Luke's version of the Sermon on the Mount, which version is generally known as
''the Sermon on the Plain'' (6:20-40). Here, Jesus' audience is not
merely the chosen twelve apostles, but rather, ''a large gathering of his
disciples'' (6:17). This gathering is instructed: ''Give to everyone who

---

[15] J. J. Jeremias, *The Parables of Jesus* (London: S.C.M., 1972), p. 185. c.f., I. H. Marshall, *Luke: Historian and Theologian*, pp. 142-3. Henry Wansbrough believes that Luke
''positively removes'' much of the old folk-tale detail for his own didatic purpose. H.
Wansbrough, ''St. Luke and Christian Ideals in an Affluent Society'', *New Blackfriars* 49
(1968), p. 584.
[16] I. H. Marshall, *The Gospel of Luke*, p. 686.

asks you, and do not ask for your property back from the man who robs you." (6:30). In addition, the crowd is advised to, "lend without any hope of return." (6:35). This last phrase, it should be noted, was to prove extraordinarily influential in terms of the future of economic thought and policy in the West.[17]

Perhaps, it is too much to suggest that radical disinvestment is being promoted in the above passages as an absolute condition of discipleship. Robert Karris, for example, writes: "As I read Luke 5:11, 28, I notice that Peter and Levi *voluntarily* left all; they were not commanded by Jesus to leave all."[18] Again, with respect to the Levi episode, Marshall suggests that this should not be taken literally, "especially since the Lucan detail that he left everything (c.f.5.11) can hardly mean that he simply left his office there and then without some formal settling of his business."[19] Marshall is also of the opinion that the command to give to everyone (6:30), "is not to be taken over-literally."[20]

Even given such readings and opinions, there is no doubting Luke's anti-capital and pro-dependence propensities, and these are again in evidence in the section of the gospel relating the journey to Jerusalem. At one point, seventy-two disciples are sent out on a mission. They are instructed: "Carry no purse, no haversack, no sandals." (10:4). Later, Jesus commands his disciples, quite unequivocally: "Sell your possessions and give alms".(12:33).[21] One chapter on from this is the stark declaration: "None of you can be my disciple unless he gives up all his possessions."(14:33). Subsequently, Jesus counsels the rich, young aristocrat: "Sell all you own and distribute the money to the poor, and you will have treasure in heaven; then come follow me."(18:22).

The cumulative effect of the foregoing directives is to suggest that investment in heaven and investment on earth are two absolutely inimical activities. This effect is heightened by Luke's comment on Jesus' parable of a man who accumulates with a view to ensuring that his long-term consumption requirements are met, but whose accumulation is rendered pointless by his death. His investment in stocks and stores has been to no avail, and Luke observes: "So it is when a man stores up treasure for himself in place of making himself rich in the sight of God."(12:21). Logically, of course, it can be argued that the rich fool

---

[17] For further discussion see, B. Gordon, "Lending at Interest: some Jewish, Greek and Christian Approaches", *History of Political Economy*, 14 (1982), pp. 406-26.

[18] R. J. Karris, "Poor and Rich: the Lukan Sitz im Leben", in C. H. Talbert (ed.), *Perspectives on Luke-Acts* (Edinburgh: Clark, 1978), p. 116.

[19] I. H. Marshall, *The Gospel of Luke*, p. 219.

[20] ibid., p. 261.

[21] There is a considerable contrast here with the Gospel of Matthew. For comment, consult, ibid., p. 531.

impoverished himself "in the sight of God" by failing to use his capital in active, employment-creating investment. However, there is nothing in the Gospel to suggest that its author was aware of any distinctions between types of investment, or, if he was aware, that they mattered to him. What mattered was the transformation of earthly capital into heavenly capital, and the *only* means of effecting that transformation was alms giving.[22]

Neither Luke's position, nor that of Jesus, it can be contended, is as radical as might appear. For example, the invitation to the rich aristocrat that he "sell all" could be regarded as a counsel of perfection, or as something directed to the particular circumstances of that individual. Again, the need for the disciples to "give up all" may be understood to refer to an attitude required of, rather than a course of action demanded from, each of them. Such an interpretation of the latter is supported by the Greek of 14:33. "Its verbs," writes Karris, "show that the proper translation should go: all disciples must be *ready* to renounce their possessions."[23] Marshall makes the same point.[24]

That Jesus did not require total disinvestment by all his adherents is illustrated by the case of the wealthy, senior tax collector, Zacchaeus (19:1-10). He welcomes the coming of Jesus who brings salvation to his house. Zacchaeus gives half of his property to the poor, but he is not asked, as was the rich, young man, to sell up everything.

In the closing chapters of Luke's gospel there are two episodes which bear directly on the issue of the use of capital. The first of these is Jesus' commendation of the poor widow who "from the little she had, has put in all she had to live on."(21:1-4). The woman's contribution to the Temple treasury has left her without any means of support. Her behaviour may be contrasted with that which Paul asks of his Christian communities in aid of the poor in Jerusalem. They are to give of their "surplus" or "abundance". They are not to render themselves destitute as does this woman.

The second, notable episode occurs on the eve of Jesus' arrest by the Temple guard. He reminds the apostles of their earlier mission where they were to go out with no capital, and then he goes on to direct: "But now if you have a purse, take it; if you have a haversack, do the same;

---

[22] c.f., R. J. Karris, "Poor and Rich", p. 120. Consult also, Raymond Brown who finds that, for Luke, "the only proper way" of employing capital is to give it to the poor. R. E. Brown, "The Pater Noster as an Eschatological Prayer", *Theological Studies*, 22 (1961), p. 201.

[23] R. J. Karris, "Poor and Rich", p. 121.

[24] I. H. Marshall, *The Gospel of Luke*, p. 594. Here, both Karris and Marshall follow J. Dupont, *Les Beautitudes* (Paris, 1969-73).

if you have no sword, sell your cloak and buy one."(22:36). It is difficult to gauge the import of this change of instructions, but it could mean that in the era to come, when Jesus is not with them as he has been, the apostles must take a radically different attitide to possessions than the one which was appropriate for their sojurn with him. The party, the type of messianic banquet they had been enjoying in his company these past months, was over.

TENSION IN LUKE

It is very difficult to be certain of what is the appropriate pattern of Christian economic behaviour according to Luke, especially where the subjects of the possession and use of capital are concerned. Luke seems to have no appreciation of the fact that capital may be employed in a variety of ways which have differing impacts on individuals and on the welfare of society as a whole. Certain passages, as we have seen, suggest in the strongest possible terms that the only course compatible with the necessary posture of complete and utter dependence on the Father is to strip oneself of all material assets. Hence, many commentators would agree with the assessment: "For Luke, then, abandonment of material possessions is integral to the life of discipleship: taught by Jesus, demonstrated by the disciples, lived out by the early church."[25]

Alternately, it can be proposed that Luke's writings, especially when the *Acts of the Apostles* is considered together with his gospel, are characterised by an unresolved tension on the subject of capital. He is not unequivocally in the camp of *James*. This is the view taken by Henry Wansbrough who writes:

> "There are, several attitudes towards material possessions and towards property to be found in Luke, between which a certain tension exists... There is a series of sayings—perhaps the most primitive layer—which shows Jesus proclaiming the gospel to the real poor and real underprivileged, not just to the poor in spirit. To these passages Luke has added his own stress on the necessity of total renunciation. But also—and here the tension begins—he shows that rich people do belong to Christ's community both in the gospel and in the Acts. It is primarily a matter of good use of wealth, for the sake of those in need."[26]

As Wansbrough's analysis suggests, the tension can be attributed, in part, to the combination of reporting and commentary by Luke, plus his awareness that many people who had not indulged in total renunciation

---

[25] Athol Gill, *Christians and the Poor* (Canberra: Zadok Centre Paper No. 9, 1979), p. 18.

[26] H. Wansbrough, "St. Luke and Christian Ideals", p. 587.

had been attracted to, and were performing a worthwhile role in, the early Church. Almost certainly, however, there are other dimensions involved. For example, if one traces the sequence of Luke's gospel, one finds that in the early chapters there is emphasis on poverty, asceticism and repentance, but there is no direct suggestion of the abandonment of possessions. Then, the mood alters after Jesus has, returned to Nazareth; unrolled the scroll of the prophet Isaiah; and, declared that, like the prophet, he has begun, "to proclaim the Lord's year of favour" (4:16-22; cf. Is. 61:1-2).

After this declaration, there emerges the new circumstances of Jesus' public ministry, which include the combination of non-ascetic table fellowship with imperatives to bestow accumulated capital on the poor. This combination is highly appropriate behaviour in the "year of favour", which is the jubilee year of *Leviticus*.[27] During that year, men rest from their accustomed toiling, enjoy the fruits of whatever Yahweh bestows on the Land, and return alienated factors of production to their former disposition among the sons of Israel.

The year of favour comes to an end, however, both with regard to its consumption and its capital aspects. Luke foreshadows the change in consumption patterns at an early stage. In reply to the charge that his disciples are not ascetics like those of John the Baptist and of the Pharisees, Jesus argues: "Surely you cannot make the bridegroom's attendants fast while the bridegroom is still with them? But the time will come, the time for the bridegroom to be taken away from them; that will be the time they will fast." (5:34-5). The actual point at which the change takes place is marked by the Last Supper (22:14-38). Here, the apostles are not commanded to fast, although there is the suggestion of hard times to come before they banquet together again with Jesus in his kingdom. Further, they are positively instructed to change their habits of the immediate past with respect to ownership and use of capital. Forsaking the "fine, careless rapture" of the jubilee year, they are now to equip themselves with personal possessions for the tasks ahead.

Yet another dimension of the tension in Luke relating to economic matters is associated with the women in his writings. At one point in Luke's gospel (and, in Luke's gospel alone), Jesus tells men to "hate" their wives (14:26). Later, Jesus promises the reward of eternal life to men who have left their wives, "for the sake of the kingdom of God." (18:28-30). In addition, the reader is left wondering about the fate of the wives and other dependants of those men who heed the call to "leave all"

---

[27] There are grounds for the view that A.D. 26-27 was a jubilee year. See, I. H. Marshall, *The Gospel of Luke*, p. 184.

or "sell all" and follow Jesus. Yet, Luke's gospel is often called the "Gospel of Women", and with good reason. In the opening chapters, for example, he features three, strong female characters in the background for Jesus and John. Male characters such as Joseph and Simeon are mere cyphers by comparison with Mary, Elizabeth, and Anna.

Given his high regard for the role which women might play in both the plan of salvation and the ordinary business of life, it is not improbable that when he was thinking of the work of the Kingdom in relation to more mundane work, Luke had in mind, as an ideal, the situation portrayed in the alphabetic poem on the perfect wife (Pr. 31:10-31). This women is entirely capable of dealing with the household's economic problem, thus releasing her husband for the more important task of administering justice. It is almost as if the micro-economics of production could be left to the wife, while the husband attended to the more macro-economic issues such as distribution of the product of the community.

Such "perfect wives" recur in Luke's writings. They are not destitute, they have not "sold all", they have not given everything to the poor. If they had done these things, they could not have furthered the work of Jesus and Paul in their travels in the manner which is described and praised. Martha of the Mary and Martha story is one such affluent, capable woman (10:38-42). Earlier in the gospel there is explicit reference to the role played by the capital of other women of means. Jesus and the apostles are supported by, "Mary surnamed the Magdalene, from whom seven demons had gone out, Joanna the wife of Herod's steward Chuza, Susanna, and several others who provided for them out of their own resources."(8:1-3). Even on his way to his execution, Jesus is accompanied by women (probably, noblewomen of Jerusalem) whose custom it was to provide pain-killing drinks to condemned men (23:27).[28]

In the section of *Acts* which deals with Paul's missions after his break with Barnabas, Luke records as the first non-Christian to welcome Paul and his message, a woman called Lydia: "a devout woman from the town of Thyatira who was in the purple-dye trade." (Acts 16:14). Lydia was, a well-to-do entrepreneur; the retail agent in Philippi for the luxury item of purple cloth as exported from Thyatira; and, mistress of a substantial household.[29] Her household became the base for the missionary efforts of Paul and Silas in the region. There is absolutely no suggestion that Lydia sells up her business, dismisses her employees, gives

---

[28] Joseph Rhymer (ed.), *The Bible in Order* (London: Darton, Longman and Todd, 1975), p. 1785.

[29] Consult, William Neil, *The Acts of the Apostles* (London: Oliphants, 1973), p. 182, 186; and, E. Haenchen, *The Acts of the Apostles*, pp. 494-5, 499.

away her money, and joins the ranks of the poor and dependent. Other women of wealth and standing, it can be added, assist Paul and Silas in Thessalonika and in Beroea (Acts 17:4, 12).

The foregoing considerations demonstrate that it is indeed over-hasty to conclude that, for Luke, abandonment of material possessions is integral to the life of discipleship. In fact, it is possible to contend that the call to thorough-going disinvestment and economic dependence applied to men only, and merely for the period of "the Lord's year of favour", the period in which Jesus was publicly and physically with his disciples. Yet, this latter contention does not sit comfortably with Luke's obvious enthusiasm for the experiment in communalism and decapitalisation by the early Christians in Jerusalem (Acts 2:44-7; 4:32-7). Such is this enthusiasm, that it could well have led him to play down the degree to which that experiment failed. Ernst Haenchen observes that, "strangely enough, Luke does not describe in Acts the great collection on which Paul spent so much trouble and exertion and which he mentions in his epistles to the Corinthians and the Romans. Only in 24:17 does he have Paul say that he has come to Jerusalem to bring offerings and alms for his people. That these alms consisted of a substantial fund collected among his congregations Luke does not indicate, and no reader could guess it from Acts if he did not know the Pauline letters."[30]

The conclusion is that Luke failed to resolve the tensions he experienced concerning discipleship and the economic problem. Personal predisposition suggested that the true disciple was concerned with that problem only in its short-run distributive aspect. Issues of production and forward-planning should be left to the Father. However, Luke's reflection on some of the sayings and actions of Jesus, on the empirical realities of the early Church, and on the role of women in the plan of salvation prevented him from writing Christian economic behaviour simply in his own image.

GOSPEL CONTRASTS WITH LUKE

The epistles of Paul do not display the degree of tension evident in Luke concerning ownership of capital, economic status, and discipleship. The same observation can be made with respect to the gospels of Matthew,

---

[30] ibid., p. 378. On the failure of the economic arrangements of the Jerusalem community, William Neil makes the interesting observation that this may have arisen, "partly because of the loss of well-to-do Hellenists by persecution". W. Neil, *The Acts of the Apostles*, pp. 145-6. This implies that those arrangements continued to be viable for a time because of the injection of significant amounts of "foreign" capital. Perhaps then, the Jerusalem Christians understood Isaiah 61: 5-6 as applying to themselves and their era.

Mark and John. Each of these allows for a more flexible understanding of Christian economic activity than does Luke. The greater flexibility can be illustrated by reference to a variety of episodes in the life of Jesus where Luke's treatment contrasts with that of one or more of the other evangelists. In this section, we will consider four such instances: the Sermon on the Mount; the Rich Young Man; the Anointing of Jesus; and, Jesus and the Children.

In the Sermon on the Mount, Luke reports that Jesus states: "How happy are you who are poor: yours is the kingdom of God." (Lk. 6:20). However at this point, *The Gospel of Matthew* reads: "How happy are the poor in spirit; theirs is the kingdom of heaven." (Mt. 5:3). Comparing the two statements, Eduard Schweizer writes:

> "Matthew has been more insightful about what Jesus said than Luke, who merely translates Jesus' dictum literally into Greek. In Luke the statement becomes simply the legalism that in heaven all conditions are reversed, so that the poor become rich and the rich become poor... Matthew wished to derail the mere mechanical response to Jesus' words (the assumption of poverty as a ticket to heaven), so he added the phrase 'in the spirit', to emphasize the inner quality of Jesus' appeal."[31]

In Luke, the words of Jesus, here, invite the equation of low economic status with high standing in terms of God's kingdom, but this is not the case in Matthew. For the latter, possession of the kingdom is associated with those who are "conscious of their need of God's help."[32] These are "the poor in spirit", and they cannot be necessarily identified with those in society who have little or no capital.[33] Maintenance of a vivid consciousness of utter dependence on the Father neither requires, nor is it ensured by, destitution.

Both Matthew and Mark may be contrasted with Luke in their treatments of the incident involving Jesus and the rich, young man (Mt. 19:16-22; Mk. 10:17-22; Lk. 18:18-25). With Luke, the man is told quite bluntly by Jesus: "Sell all you own and distribute the money to the poor." (Lk. 18:22). Jesus seems to be confronting him with an "either-or" in regard to discipleship. However, the Jesus of the Gospel of Matthew states: "If you wish to be perfect, go and sell what you own and

---

[31] E. Schweizer, *The Good News According to Matthew* (London: S.P.C.K., 1978), p. 88, c.f., A. H. McNeile, *The Gospel According to St. Matthew* (London: Macmillan, 1961), p. 50; and, Alexander Jones, "The Gospel of Jesus Christ According to St. Matthew", in B. Orchard et al., *A Catholic Commentary on Holy Scripture* (London: Nelson, 1953), p. 861.

[32] David M. Stanley, *The Gospel of St. Matthew* (Collegeville, Minn.: Liturgical Press, 1963), p. 36.

[33] Pierre Biard has observed that for Jesus, "poverty extends infinitely farther than the simple socio-economic situation of material indigence." P. Biard, "Biblical Teaching on Poverty", *Cross Currents*, 14 (1964), p. 438.

give the money to the poor." (Mt. 19:21). The significance of this verse has been remarked by William Davies. He writes:

> "...Matthew has introduced the idea that there are grades of achievement in the Christian life. The counsel to sell all and give to the poor is designed only for the perfect: It is not meant to be applied to all. The point of this passage is not to introduce into the church two orders of morality but to recognize that the commandment of Jesus discriminates; it respects individual differences among men."[34]

That the issue at hand is one of individual capacity and of degree, is also brought out by Mark's exposition of the same incident. With Mark as with Matthew, it is not a question of "either-or". It is not a question of the approbation of Jesus *versus* the retention of the ownership and control of capital.

Mark recounts that when the young man confronts Jesus and attests both his respect for Jesus as a teacher and his devotion to Mosaic observance, "Jesus looked steadily at him and loved him, and he said, 'There is one thing you lack. Go and sell everything you own and give the money to the poor, and you will have treasure in heaven; then come, follow me.'" (Mk. 10:21). From this, it is clear that the man's existing command of wealth has not prevented him from becoming an admirable person, but Jesus believes that he has not yet realised his full potential. John O'Flynn comments: "The man was good and sincere, but it was still possible for him to aim higher by carrying out a counsel of perfection."[35]

The divergent treatments by Mark and Luke of the immediate sequel to this episode are also indicative of the gulf between the two evangelists on ownership of capital and the following of Christ (Mk. 10:23-27; Lk. 18:24-27). In Mark, the rich man refuses Jesus' invitation and goes sadly on his way. This leads Jesus into dialogue with his disciples on the subject of entry into the kingdom of God. Jesus asserts the impossibility for any man—*rich or poor*—to find a place in the kingdom by virtue of what he is. Entry is something which only God can effect for any individual.

With Luke, however, the Marcan story undergoes radical changes which alter its meaning in a thorough-going fashion. The story is turned into a discourse on the near absolute incompatibility of temporal command of wealth with personal salvation. In the first place, Luke alters Mark's account by having Jesus direct his initial remarks about the

---

[34] W. D. Davies, *The Sermon on the Mount* (Cambridge: Cambridge University Press, 1969), p. 111. c.f., E. Schweizer, *The Good News*, p. 388; and, A. H. McNeile, *The Gospel According to St. Matthew*, p. 279.

[35] J. O'Flynn, The Gospel of Jesus Christ according to St. Mark", in, B. Orchard et al., ibid., p. 921.

kingdom to the young man rather than to the disciples. Then, as Howard Marshall has noted:

> "Luke omits reference to the disciples as the participants in the discussion, and thereby makes it clear that the comments of Jesus are to be understood as directed to non-disciples, attempting to stir them up to realise the danger of riches. So Mk. 10:24 disappears with the disciples' surprise and the consequent repetition of Jesus' statement. This means that the conversation is concerned solely with the rich, and the general comment on the impossibility of anybody entering the kingdom disappears."[36]

Luke's special attachment to poverty and disinvestment is also illustrated by his omission of sayings and actions of Jesus which might be construed as running counter to this personal bias. A case in point here is his account of the anointing of Jesus at the table by a woman, an event which is related in the Gospel of John as well as in all three synoptic gospels (Mt. 26:6-13; Mk. 14:3-9; Lk. 7:36-50; Jn. 11:55-12:11). Each of the non-Lucan texts feature a difference of opinion between Jesus and his disciples as part of this incident. The difference concerns the use of capital, but the matter is not remarked by Luke.

Put briefly, the circumstance is that of Jesus resting and dining in a household when a woman enters and pours expensive oil on his body. Matthew reports the reactions of Jesus and his Disciples, as follows:

> "When they saw this, the disciples were indignant; 'Why this waste?' they said. This could have been sold at a high price and the money given to the poor." Jesus noticed this. 'Why are you upsetting the woman?' he said to them. "What she has done for me is one of the good works indeed! You have the poor with you always, but you will not always have me. When she poured this ointment on my body, she did it to prepare me for burial." (Mt. 26:8-12).

Here, there is a clear contradiction by Jesus of the proposition that the only legitimate use of capital is its liquidation for conversion into alms. The contradiction is expressed in virtually identical words in Mark (14:4-8), while in John, the legitimacy of Jesus' position is emphasised by putting the charge of neglect of the poor into the mouth of the traitor Judas Iscariot rather than "the disciples". (Jn. 12:4-8).

Nothing of this emerges from Luke's gospel. There is no dispute over the employment of capital, and Luke turns the anointing into a lesson

---

[36] I. H. Marshall, *The Gospel of Luke*, p. 686. For further discussion, consult, J. D. M. Derrett, "A Camel through the Eye of a Needle", *New Testament Studies*, 32, 3 (July 1986), 465-70. See also, J. D. M. Derrett, *The Making of Mark*, Vol. 2 (Shipston: Drinkwater, 1985), 172-77.

[37] c.f., J. M. Creed, *The Gospel According to St. Luke* (London: Macmillan, 1965), pp. 109-10.

concerning the character of Jesus' mission in relation to tax collectors and sinners.[37] Such are the differences between Luke and the other writers that some biblical commentators specualte that he must be describing a different incident.[38] However, it may also be proposed that the omission of the debate concerning the ointment is deliberate on Luke's part. Jesus' position (especially if Luke was not very familiar with Jewish custom) was difficult to reconcile with his own. Further, even if Luke was describing a different incident, there is the question of why he omits the one which he could well have had before him in the text of Mark.

Another set of omissions which may be due to Luke's special position on Christian economic activity occurs in his presentation of the story of Jesus and the Children. This is found in each of the synoptic gospels (Mk. 10:13-16; Mt. 19:13-15; Lk. 18:15-17). The text of Mark states:

> "People were bringing little children to him, for him to touch them. The disciples turned them away, but when Jesus saw this he was indignant and said to them, 'Let the little children come to me; do not stop them; for it is to such as these that the kingdom of God belongs. I tell you solemnly, anyone who does not welcome the kingdom of God like a little child will never enter it.' Then he put his arms round them and gave them his blessing." (Mk. 10:13-16).

The Gospel of Matthew conveys the same detail, but this is not the case with Luke. The latter omits, Jesus indignation at the behaviour of his disciples; the embracing of the children; and (most significantly, perhaps) Jesus' blessing of them. Why these omissions? Perhaps, it is because Luke wishes to, "supress those details of Mark's Gospel which risk compromising the exalted holiness of Jesus in the minds of Gentile readers."[39] Rather more likely however (and more consistent with the emphases of his Gospel), is that Luke wishes to reduce as much as possible the force of the suggestion in the above that the true disciple of Jesus can be engaged in the ordinary business of family life with its customary social and economic involvements.

The foregoing verses represent a strong affirmation by Jesus that assumption of the responsibilities of fatherhood is quite compatible with a man's following him. That affirmation has been noted by William Davies. He writes that here we find,

> "concern to understand what the moral demands of Jesus imply. Did they allow for the bringing up of children? Could one who was to take as his aim

---

[38] See, e.g., A. H. McNeile, *The Gospel According to St. Matthew*, p. 376; C. Stuhlmueller, *The Gospel of Saint Luke*, p. 71; and, R. E. Brown, *The Gospel of St. John and the Johannine Epistles* (Collegeville, Minn.: Liturgical Press, 1965), pp. 61-2.

[39] C. Stuhlmueller, *The Gospel of Saint Luke*, p. 120.

the kind of indifference to toil and labour that we find in the lily of the field—could he assume the responsibilities of fatherhood? The disciples are tempted to a negative answer, but their Lord reassures them.''[40]

Bringing children to Jesus, then, is one of the works which serve the kingdom. Further, it is a work with a variety of economic implications including the need for family capital and attention to the mundane business of production. It implies that the economic activity of at least some of Jesus' followers can extend beyond that of a single-minded attempt to achieve a more equitable communal distribution of consumption goods in the short-run.

Such implications posed a decided threat to Luke's conception of what ought be involved in discipleship. To meet it, he not only omitted key aspects of the Marcan detail, but he changed the context of the entire episode, as Howard Marshall explains. Marshall writes:

> "In Mark it (Jesus and the Children) forms part of a series of incidents giving teaching of Jesus in respect of marriage, children and possessions (Mk. 10:1-12, 13-16, 17-31); here (i.e., in Luke) it is part of a series describing what is involved in becoming a disciple... Luke's interest in the pericope is more with children as an example to adults.''[41]

The fact that the sense of this and other stories is so different as between Mark and Luke raises the general issue of their literary relationship. A majority of modern scholars hold to the view that Mark's gospel was a basic source for Luke.[42] Yet there must be some doubt about the view, unless it is allowed that Luke was quite ruthless with the text before him when it came to his promoting an anti-Marcan, non-Matthean, non-Pauline line on the limits of the economic behaviour allowable for followers of Jesus.

That Luke's interpretation of the message of Jesus is somewhat peculiar in terms of most of the rest of the New Testament has come to be recognized by a number of commentators. Karl Schelkle, for example, observes:

> "The relationship of the Christian to possessions was, for this evangelist, a pressing problem. Therefore he collected such particularized traditions as were available to him, probably even sharpened criticism which he came upon in the sources he utilized, as is indicated by Synoptic comparison with Matthew and Mark... The imitation of Jesus is the fulfillment of the requirement of poverty. Luke emphasizes (5:11, 28; 18:22): 'They left *everything*' (while Mark 1:18, 20; 2:14; 10:21 consistently says only that

---

[40] W. D. Davies, *The Sermon on the Mount*, p. 111.
[41] I. H. Marshall, *The Gospel of Luke*, pp. 681-2.
[42] See, W. G. Kummel, *Introduction to the New Testament* (17th edition; Nashville: Abingdon, 1975), pp. 132-47.

those who were called followed him). Only in Luke is the disciple bidden to dispose of his possessions in alms."[43]

Luke's writings, it is clear, must be approached with caution by anyone attempting to employ biblical literature to generalise on "the Christian approach" to economic life. This is not to deny, however, that those writings were to exercise a profound influence on the future of economic thought. Not a few of the well educated pagans who were converted to Christianity at a mature age and became "Fathers of the Church" found Luke's peculiar position most amenable to their preconceptions.

---

[43] K. H. Schelkle, *Theology of the New Testament*, Vol. III, p. 309. For a quite different understanding, consult, Thomas E. Schmidt, *Hostility to Wealth in the Synoptic Gospels* (Sheffield: JSOT Press, 1987). However, see also, D. L. Mealand, *Poverty and Expectation in the Gospels* (London: SPCK, 1980), and Luke T. Johnson, *The Literary Function of Possessions in Luke-Acts* (Missoula: Scholars Press, 1977).

CHAPTER SEVEN

JERUSALEM, ROME, AND ALEXANDRIA

> "The faithful all lived together and owned everything in common; they sold their goods and possessions and shared out the proceeds among themselves according to what each one needed."
>
> *Acts of the Apostles*, 2:44-45.

> "We must not cast away riches which can benefit our neighbour. Possessions were made to be possessed; goods are called goods because they do good, and they have been provided by God for the good of men: they are at hand and serve as the material, the instruments for a good use in the hand of him who knows how to use them. If you use them with skill you reap the benefit from them."
>
> Clement of Alexandria, *Who Is the Rich Man That Shall be Saved?*, XIV.

The official legitimation of Christianity within the Roman Empire did not eventuate until the Emperor Constantine issued his Edict of Milan in A.D.313. Very rapidly thereafter, Christians rose to power and prominence in temporal affairs, and leading minds of the Church were obliged to address social issues on a scale which their predecessors had not confronted. The post-Constantinan response is considered in the next chapter. Here, we are concerned with a range of reactions to the economic problem during the centuries in which the emerging Church struggled with the challenges of, minority status; recurring persecution, and its initial attempts to understand what the life of Jesus of Nazareth meant.

THE JERUSALEM COMMUNITY

One of the most celebrated aspects of the economic behaviour of early Christians is related to practices of the primitive Church in Jerusalem during the short span between the execution of Jesus and the destruction of the Second Temple in A.D.70. The Jerusalem community appears to have been involved in an experiment in communalism, and its members engaged in voluntary decapitalisation to a substantial extent. According to the *Acts of the Apostles* (which might be idealizing the past):

> "The whole group of believers was united, heart and soul; no one claimed for his own use anything that he had, as everything they owned was held

in common... None of their members was ever in want, as all those who owned land or houses would sell them, and bring the money from them, to present it to the apostles; it was then distributed to any members who might be in need." (Acts 4:32, 34-35; see also, 2:44-45).

Not surprisingly, the progressive decapitalisation soon led to the community's inability to cope with scarcity by means of its own resources. There is the suggestion in *Acts* that the onset of destitution may have been reinforced by members of the community forsaking their normal, productive avocations: "They went as a body to the Temple every day." (Acts 2:46). Such was the plight of the Jerusalem community at an early stage, that when the apostle Paul sought its sanction for his missionary activities, permission was forthcoming only on the condition that he raise funds to help sustain the faltering experiment in train.

Paul recounts the foregoing in his letter to the *Galatians*. He writes: "So, James, Cephas and John, these leaders, these pillars, shook hands with Barnabas and me as a sign of partnership: we were to go to the pagans and they to the circumcised. The only thing they insisted on was that we should remember to help the poor, as indeed I was anxious to do." (Ga.2:9-10). As a result of this pledge, Paul was to divert a good deal of his time and energy to raising money for "the saints" in Jerusalem. This irksome diversion, it can be remarked, may help explain the character of the economics of the Pauline epistles. At no stage does Paul advise his congregations to emulate the practice of the mother church. Quite the reverse. The communities for which he feels responsible are not to make their incorporation in Christ an occasion for a plunge into experimentation with economic relationships. Not only are their members to maintain steady and devoted application to work, but also they are not to engage in any dramatic liquidation of capital. Nowhere does Paul even suggest common ownership or pooling of possessions. As Alan Richardson observes, Paul, "who had had to organize relief-collections for the 'poor saints' in Jerusalem had already had first-hand acquaintance with the disastrous economic consequences of mistaken eschatological notions...".[1]

The "disastrous economic consequences" of the Jerusalem experiment, it can be added, were not acknowledged by St. Luke, who wrote *Acts*. A convert from paganism, Luke was anxious to equate Christian living with voluntary poverty (as is abundantly illustrated in the same writer's gospel). Hence, as Ernst Haenchen writes, "Luke does not describe in Acts the great collection on which Paul spent so much trouble and exertion and which he mentions in his epistles to the Corinthians and

---

[1] A. Richardson, *The Biblical Doctrine of Work* (London: S.C.M., 1958), p. 39.

the Romans. Only in 24:17 does he have Paul say that he has come to Jerusalem to bring offerings and alms for his people. That these alms consisted of a substantial fund collected among his congregations Luke does not indicate, and no reader could guess it from Acts if he did not know the Pauline letters."[2]

THE WEALTH OF NATIONS

Why did the Jerusalem Christians decapitalise, communalise, and come to rely on the financial support of foreigners? A popular, modern explanation is that the community lived in the expectation of an early second coming of Christ which would make the existing economic order obsolete. Almost certainly, this explanation is incorrect, especially as there is no evidence that any of the other urban Christian communities behaved in the same manner. Again, the contemporary letters of St. Paul to some of those other communities show that he was anxious to dissociate Christian living from the current of apocalyptic fervour which was still a feature of speculation in the Near East. He encouraged each of his "brothers" to "stay as he was before God at the time of his call." (1 Co. 7:24). Paul informed the Thessalonians: "You will not be expecting us to write anything to you, brothers, about 'times and seasons', since you know very well that the day of the Lord is going to come like a thief in the night." (1 Th. 5:1-2; see also, 2 Th. 2:1f). Would St. Paul have been so entirely out of sympathy with the "leaders" and "pillars" of Jerusalem as to take this stance when they were encouraging their brothers to take a quite different view?

To appreciate the position of the Jerusalem community, it is helpful to reflect that they had not been presented by the Master with a blueprint for social organisation. In contrast with some of the reformers of antiquity, such as the Socratic philosophers, Jesus had eschewed social engineering.[3] However, one of the leaders of the Jerusalem community, Peter, entertained no doubt as to the function of his fellows. They were,

> "a chosen race, a royal priesthood, a consecrated nation, a people set apart to sing the praises of God who called you out of darkness into his wonderful light." (1 P.2:9).

---

[2] E. Haenchen, *The Acts of the Apostles, a Commentary* (Oxford: Blackwell, 1971), p. 378.

[3] C. F., H. Conzelmann, *Jesus* (Philadelphia: Fortress, 1975), p. 66; G. Ernest Wright, *The Biblical Doctrine of Man in Society* (London: S.C.M., 1954), p. 147; Eduard Lohse, *Colossians and Philemon* (Philadelphia: Fortress, 1971), p. 156; W. D. Davies and D. Daube (eds.), *The Background of the New Testament and its Eschatology* (Cambridge: Cambridge University Press, 1964), p. 101; and, Oscar Cullman, *The Early Church* (London: S.C.M., 1956), p. 195.

This priestly status (although not exclusive to Jewish Christians) had immediate implications in terms of social organization for Jews, especially if they were living in Jerusalem whilst the Temple still stood. Hence, *Acts* portrays the life of the community as turning around the Temple, plus table fellowship and care for the material needs of the poor as had been recommended by the life and teachings of Jesus.

Abandonment of personal capital in the form of land and houses (in rural areas, at least) was in direct accord with assumption of priestly office, since, traditionally, priests possessed no landed property. Further, it was entirely in line with tradition that a priest's sustenance was derived from the resources of the faith-community at large, rather than by his taking up productive avocations.[4] Hence, the new faith-community pooled its possessions, and, probably, forsook former activities for the mediatory role which is the essence of priesthood.

It also seems highly probable that the new race of priests would not have found it anomolous when the resources of the immediate community began to prove inadequate for their support. The new priesthood was not merely mediating between God and the Jews, but rather, between God and the members of all nations. It could well have understood its economic problem in terms of the Solution by Mediation (see, Chapter Three). As Isaiah had predicted:

> "Strangers will be there to feed your flocks, foreigners as your ploughmen and vinedressers; but you, you will be named 'priests of Yahweh', they will call you 'ministers of our God.' You will feed on the wealth of nations and array yourselves in their magnificence." (Is. 61:5-6).

The particular circumstances which marked the transition of the Jerusalem community from reliance on decapitalisation to funding from abroad is not clear. There is a reference to famine in *Acts* (11:27-30), but the reference is too vague to designate this as a definite turningpoint.[5] One interesting possibility is suggested by William Neil's observation that, "the mother church in Jerusalem was notoriously poor, partly perhaps because of the pooling of resources in the early days, and partly

---

[4] On the priest's "portion" and the Levite's "portion", see, *The Book of Numbers* 18:8-32. Duncan Derrett observes that in the Last Supper, "Jesus is also acting as if a second Moses inducting a new priesthood". J. D. M. Derrett, "The Upper Room and the Dish", *Heythrop Journal*, 26, 4 (Oct. 1985), p. 379.

[5] C.f., F. J. Foakes Jackson and Kirsopp Lake, *The Acts of the Apostles*, Vol. IV (1932; Grand Rapids, Michigan: Baker, 1979), pp. 130-132. Another hypothesis could be that the Jerusalem community came to attract an unusually high proportion of economically dependent persons as compared with those who were able and willing to be self-sufficient. However, there is no textual evidence for this.

because of the loss of well-to-do Hellenists by persecution."[6] Given that
the "Hellenists" were Greek-speaking Jewish Christians from abroad, it
would seem that the economic viability of the Jerusalem experiment
could have been dependent from a very early stage on "the wealth of
nations."

In any event, it is clear that the Jerusalem case was a unique one
among urban communities in the early Church.[7] Further, it was never
intended to provide a general model for the economic organisation of
other Christian communities, and when the Temple was destroyed its
particular rationale was at an end. Nevertheless, the case is an important
one in that some influential writers of later centuries were prone to refer
to this model as the exemplar of the ideal in socio-economic behaviour
for Christians in general.[8]

NOT OF THIS WORLD

The pre-Constantine Fathers of the Church do not present a united front
on questions of the economic engagements of Christians. In fact, there
is a notable divergence of approach involving some of the most able of
early patristic authors. This divergence has been observed by Oscar
Cullman who writes:

> "The books of the New Testament contain hardly any precise information
> on the relations which the disciples of Christ are to maintain towards the
> civilization, culture and institutions of the ancient world ... From the
> second century, however, the situation changes. Among Christian writers,
> some like Tatian and Tertullian were to fulminate against pagan civiliza-

---

[6] William Neil, *The Acts of the Apostles* (London: Oliphants, 1973), pp. 145-146. The
custom of donations to Jerusalem by non-resident Christian Jews may represent the continuation of a standard Jewish practice whereby money was sent for Passover expenses
and for the temple service. Perhaps, the non-resident Christians understood themselves
to be contributing to "the New Temple" (of prophecy). This new temple, as Bullough
points out, is interpreted, "not merely as the centre of Jewish worship, but as a type of
the universal Church of Christ, wither all nations will come to adore." S. Bullough,
"Aggeus (Haggai)", in, B. Orchard et al., *A Catholic Commentary on Holy Scripture* (London: Nelson, 1953), p. 687.

[7] A factor which might have contributed to Jerusalem's singularity was the survival
of "an ideal of encratism". Jean Danielou writes: "This ideal seems to be connected with
a Jewish pietist and more particularly an Essene milieu, and to have been adopted by
John the Baptist. Although it was set aside by Christ, there is evidence that it persisted
in the Jerusalem community, and especially in the person of its bishop James.' *A History
of Early Christian Doctrine*, Vol. I (London: Darton, Longman and Todd, 1964), p. 373.

[8] "The interest in the model community of Jerusalem has been constantly present in
the mind of many church reformers, from the early centuries through Basil and
Augustine to the Middle Ages." Paul J. Fedwick, *The Church and the Charisma of Leadership
in Basil of Caesarea* (Toronto: Pontifical Institute of Mediaeval Studies, 1979), p. 24.

tion, whilst others, the apologists, and, above all, Clement of Alexandria, were to apply themselves to reconciling the achievements of pagan culture with the demands of the gospel.''[9]

In this section we consider the anti-engagement stance as represented by Tertullian. This stance is contrasted with that of Clement, in the following portion of the chapter.

Tertullian, a brilliant Carthaginian lawyer who practised in Rome was born in A.D.160 when the Roman Empire was at the pinnacle of its power and magnificence. During his lifetime he was witness to the beginnings of the long decline of that Empire. As early as 193 (the accession of Septimus Severus) economic difficulties were becoming evident, and these multiplied during Tertullian's mature years. Also throughout his lifetime, he experienced the suspicion, and even hostility, displayed by many of his fellow citizens towards the growing number of Christians in their midst. In 202, Septimus Severus went so far as to forbid the baptism of any more pagans. Given such an environment, and Tertullian's personal inclination to an extremely puritanical code of conduct, he became an "outsider". Of Tertullian and his like-minded contemporaries, Georges Florovsky writes:

> "They were socially committed and engaged in the Church, and not in the world. "For us nothing is more alien than public affairs' declared Tertullian (*Apologeticum*, 38.3). 'I have withdrawn myself from the society', he said on another occasion (*De Pallio*, 5). Christians were in this sense 'outside society', voluntary outcasts and outlaws,—outside of the social order of this world."[10]

Tertullian took a dim view of contemporary society, and an even dimmer view of its future in secular terms. In his *De Anima*, he observes that, "the world itself, as it appears to our eyes, becomes more refined and progresses from day to day." Yet, the reality is that, "we are now a burden on the world, there are barely enough of the essentials for us, our needs have become more acute, and there is a cry of complaint on the lips of all men, for nature can no longer sustain us." He predicts that in the future, "epidemics, famines, wars and the earth's opening to swallow whole cities" will serve to help correct the population-resources imbalance.[11]

---

[9] O. Cullman, loc.cit.

[10] G. Florovsky, "Empire and Desert: Antinomies of Christian History", *Greek Orthodox Theological Review*, 3 (1957), pp. 134-135.

[11] *De Anima*, XXX, P.L.II, 700. The Malthusian sentiment of Tertullian is also found in other writers of the period. Cyprian of Carthage (200-258), in arguing that Christians should be celibate, contends that the world is now full (*De Habitu Virginum*, XXIII P.L. iv, 475). Earlier, the Greek apologist Bishop Theophilus of Antioch (d.181) also claimed that a population maximum had been attained (*Ad. Autolycum* II, 32).

When defending fellow Christians against contemporary pagan criticisms, Tertullian did not hesitate to emphasise the role which those Christians were playing in the economic and social concerns of the Empire. Tertullian protested,

"we sojourn with you in the world, abjuring neither forum, nor shambles, nor bath, nor booth, nor inn, nor weekly market, nor any other places of commerce... We sail with you, and fight with you, and till the ground with you; and in like manner we unite with you in your traffickings—even in the various arts we make public property of our works for your benefit." (*Apology*, xlii).

However, where politics is concerned, Tertullian's tone is decidely different. He affirms: "As those in whom all ardour in the pursuit of honour and glory is dead, we have no pressing inducement to take part in your public meetings; nor is there aught more entirely foreign to us than affairs of state." (*Apology*, xxxviii). Christians, it would seem, are quite prepared to leave the broad decisions shaping the future of society to the pagans in whose world the Christians happen to find themselves. This particular abjuration of social responsibility may be merely a tactical ploy on Tertullian's part, but it is in marked contrast with the attitude of some of the later Fathers.

As for the productive engagements of Christians, Tertullian is deeply suspicious of any involvements in trade and commerce. Such involvements create occasions for duplicity, and they imply covetousness which is akin to idolatory. (*On Idolatry*, XI). Even more emphatically, Christians are precluded from financial avocations. Like almost all the other Christian writers of the patristic centuries, Tertullian is totally opposed to the taking of interest on loans (*Against Marcion*, 4, 17). However, he goes further than most:

"In his eyes not only does the prohibition of usury [in the Old Testament] remain, but it is now overshadowed by a call that goes beyond it—not even to seek the principal from one who is in need."[12]

Tertullian recommends contempt for wealth, and patience as one loses it (*On Patience*, 7, 2). He is also an enthusiast for Christians adopting a communal approach to the use of possessions. At one point he even states that his own community had, "all things in common except wives." (*Apology*, xxxix). This phrase might be taken to suggest that Tertullian's rejection of the world of Rome extended to his living in a communistic

---

[12] R. P. Maloney, "The Teaching of the Fathers on Usury", *Vigiliae Christianne*, 27 (1973), p. 244. A survey of the earlier Judeo-Christian tradition on interest-taking is, Barry Gordon, "Lending at Interest: Some Jewish, Greek and Christian Approaches, 800 B.C.—A.D.100", *History of Political Economy*, 14 (1982), pp. 406-426.

enclave. Yet such an inference is almost certainly incorrect. The context affirms the principle of communal use, but not communal ownership.

Tertullian's refusal to develop a positive strategy for Christian engagement in contemporary economic life was not the result of ignorance on his part concerning that life. To the contrary, there are incidental passages in his writings which reveal a keen, analytical ability in respect of economic processes. These passages include: observations of the roles of product demand, determination of wage rates, and labour mobility (*On Idolatry*, VIII); and, analysis of the factors determining economic value (*De Cultu Feminarum*, I and II).[13] The basis for Tertullian's refusal was a deeply experienced combination of alienation and hope. As Christopher Dawson writes:

> "His work is marked by a spirit of fierce and indomitable hostility to the whole tradition of pagan civilization, both social and intellectual. He has no desire to minimize the opposition between the Church and the Empire, for all his hopes are fixed on the passing of the present order and the coming of the Kingdom of the Saints."[14]

Something of the same spirit infuses such early post-apostolic works as *The Teaching of the Twelve*, *The Shepherd of Hermas*, *The Epistle of Barnabas*, and the *First Epistle of Clement*. These too, "present Christianity as a way of life quite separate from culture."[15] However, these are less vehment and less overtly confrontationist than the writings of Tertullian.

CHRISTIAN ENGAGEMENT

Alexandria was the greatest commercial city of the Roman Empire.[16] Further, it was a major centre for the establishment of an interface between Christianity and pagan philosophy. Pantaenus (d.216), who was a Stoic, was among the founders of a Christian catechetical school in the city.[17] One of Pantaenus' students, Clement (150-215), succeeded his

---

[13] The analytical quality of these passages has been remarked in, Joseph B. Hubbard, *Economic Thought in Patristic Literature* (unpublished Doctoral thesis, Harvard University, 1923), see esp., p. 133; pp. 145-6; and p. 173.

[14] C. Dawson, *The Dynamics of World History* (New York: Mentor Omega Books, 1962), pp. 296-297.

[15] H. Richard Niebuhr, *Christ and Culture* (New York: Harper, 1951), p. 49.

[16] A. H. M. Jones, *The Roman Economy* (Oxford: Blackwell, 1974), p. 59.

[17] "The desire to counteract eccentric and heretical tendencies in the Egyptian Church may have played its part in the establishment of the Catechetical School of Alexandria, but the principal motive was no doubt to provide for Christians a means of higher education other than that of the pagan university in the Museum." H. Idris Bell, *Cults and Creeds in Graeco-Roman Egypt* (Liverpool: Liverpool University Press, 1953), p. 96. On the origins of the school consult also, E. F. Osborn, *The Philosophy of Clement of Alexandria* (London: Cambridge University Press, 1957).

teacher as head of the school and went on to effect a synthesis between the Christian "way" and post-Socratic intellectualism. This synthesis proved extremely influential in terms of subsequent patristic thought. Clement, it has been observed,

> "was the first to construct a large philosophy of Christian doctrine, with a recognition of the conventional limits, but by the help and in the domain of Greek thought."[18]

His construction is heavily Stoic with respect to moral conduct.[19] However, as a Christian living in a cosmopolitan environment, and with first-hand knowledge of a sophisticated regional economy, Clement is prepared to demonstrate how both the Stoic and New Testament canons can be satisfied without a Tertullian-like withdrawal from contemporary culture.

Fundamental for Clement's understanding of the economic activity of Christians is a distinction between the ownership and use of capital. The distinction is grounded in a stewardship theory of property. Clement writes:

> "But we say that the goods of this earth are the property of another, not as an absurdity, or as if they were not things of God, the Lord of all, but since we do not remain in them for all eternity. By possession they are other peoples, and become theirs by possession; by use they are the property of each one of us, through whom they come into being, but only in so far as it is necessary to be one with us." (*Stromata*, IV, 13).

From this, it is apparent, Christians can participate freely in the process of accumulating capital, provided that they are prepared to use that capital as if its ownership is common. Clement's position is encouraging for the entrepreneurial aspects of the economic life with which he was familiar in Alexandria. However, it finds no room for the rentiers of his world. He challenges the rentiers with the example of Jesus: "For each of us he gave his life—the equivalent for all. This he demands of us in return, to give our lives for one another. And if we owe our lives to the brethren and have made such a mutual compact with the Saviour, why should we any more hoard and shut up wordly goods, which are beggarly, foreign to us, and transitory." (*Who is the Rich Man That Shall be Saved?*, xxxvii).

Clement's solution for the economic problem on the individual level is quite unambiguous. The main strategy in contesting scarcity is

---

[18] Edwin Hatch, *The Influence of Greek Ideas on Christianity* (New York: Harper, 1957), p. 323.

[19] C.f., H. Richard Niebuhr, op.cit., p. 125; and, Henry Chadwick, *Early Christian Thought and the Classical Tradition* (Oxford: Clarendon, 1966), p. 42.

rational adjustment of consumption. "The best wealth", he observes, "is to have few desires." (*The Tutor*, II, 3). This recommendation, however, does not constitute advocacy of voluntary poverty. Clement has no time for poverty, whether voluntary or involuntary.[20] He writes:

> "For neither great nor worthy to be desired is the state of one so lacking in possessions that he does not have wherewith to live; for if it were, then that whole swarm of proletarians, derelicts and beggars who live from hand to mouth, all those wretched cast out upon the streets, though they live in ignorance of God and of his justice, would be the most blessed and the most religious and the only candidates for eternal life simply because they are penniless and find it hard to live, lacking the most modest means." (*Who is the Rich Man That Shall be Saved?*, XI).

In fact, Clement regards poverty as a major obstacle to an individual's development as a person. He contends that, "The possession of the necessities of life keep the soul free and independent if it knows how to use earthly goods wisely ... We must be busy with material concerns not for themselves, but for the body, the care of which is required by the very care of the soul, to which all things must tend." (*Stromata*, IV, 5).

Given this outlook, Clement is happy to have Christians actively involved in the bustling commercial life of Alexandria. He assures those Christians that, "it is not at all forbidden to busy oneself with an unwordly mind with wordly things according to the will of God." (*The Tutor*, III, 11). By busying themselves in productive activities, Christians will be able to command the necessities that help keep them free and independent as persons. Further, success in their economic engagements will put them in a better position to come to the aid of their fellow citizens.

In his development of this latter theme, Clement strikes a rare (perhaps, unique) note in the economic thought of early Christianity. From the very beginning it had been a hallmark of Christianity to stress the necessity of caring for the material needs of the poor to an extent and in a manner for which there were no equivalents in local pagan cultures.[21] Yet, the dedication of Christians to the material relief of

---

[20] C.f., Robert M. Grant, *Early Christianity and Society* (London: Collins, 1978), p. 108.

[21] Demetrios Constantelos, for example, observes that, "philanthropia in Greek antiquity depended mostly on the policies of those in charge of the government. When their treasuries were exhausted, all forms of public assistance generally collapsed. As a rule no underlying and widespread spirit of philanthropia prevailed ... While philanthropia in the ancient Greek world was mostly anthropocentric, in Christianity it became eminently theocentric. The principle of philanthropy was the love of God rather than the love of man." D. J. Constantelos, *Byzantine Philanthropy and Social Welfare* (New Brunswick, N. J.: Rutgers University Press, 1968), p. 11. See also, A. H. M. Jones, *The Later Roman Empire, 284-602*, Vol. 2 (Oxford: Blackwell, 1964), p. 971.

others was understood simply in terms of the unremitting obligation to almsgiving. Clement, however, suggests that the relief of others will depend, in part, on the ways in which Christians use their capital apart from the liquidation of that capital for charitable distributions. He affirms:

> "We must not cast away riches which can benefit our neighbour. Possessions were made to be possessed; goods are called goods because they do good, and they have been provided by God for the good of men: they are at hand and serve as the material, the instruments for a good use in the hand of him who knows how to use them. If you use them with skill you reap the benefit from them." (*Who is the Rich Man That Shall be Saved?*, XIV).

Here, Clement seems to have grasped the fact that concerned entrepreneurs with capital may be able to do much more for the poor in economic terms than if those same entrepreneurs are themselves living from hand to mouth. This insight, which appears to have escaped the other Fathers, is probably attributable to Clement's acquaintance with an unusually sophisticated economic environment of the kind that was remote from the experience of most other leading thinkers of Christian antiquity. In that environment, capital and entrepreneurship performed social roles which were anything but apparent in the regional rural economies or governmental administrative centres which afforded the social settings for the lives and work of those others. Alexandria was a rare milieu in an Empire where agriculture accounted for all but five per cent of total annual income.[22]

Clement's insights concerning the potential roles of capital and entrepreneurship in a Christian economic order were not taken up by later Fathers. Hence, it is understandable that Jacob Viner complains: "No Father seems to have recognised the possibility that income or property in excess of current need might help the poor more if used productively to provide them with cheap necessaries or with remunerative employment than if distributed as alms."[23] However, a number of these

---

[22] A. H. M. Jones, *The Roman Economy* (Oxford: Blackwell, 1974), p. 138.

[23] J. Viner, "The Economic Doctrines of the Christian Fathers", *History of Political Economy*, 10 (1978), p. 23. For a modern economist, it is difficult to appreciate just how "primitive" the Roman economy remained despite the size and geographical scope which it attained. On the rudimentary character of that economy, see, Raymond W. Goldsmith, *Premodern Financial Systems* (Cambridge: Cambridge University Press, 1987), pp. 34-59. In the light of Goldsmith's study, the failure of the Fathers, in general, to perceive a social role for investment is quite explicable. Another aspect of this study, which should be remarked, is its demonstration of the extraordinary degree of concentration of wealth and income (by modern standards) exhibited by the Roman and most other ancient economies. Old Testament, New Testament, and Patristic economic thought must be appreciated in terms of that concentration, and, in the light of the expectation

later Fathers were very concerned with the incidence of scarcity and its effects. Their remedy for dealing with the economic problem may be termed, the Solution by Charity.

---

that the huge gulf between the tiny minority of ''rich'' and the remainder of the populace could be bridged only sporadically by individual initiatives from particular members of the minority. In these circumstances, receipt of charity by the poor was not in the least demeaning for its recipients. Further, the ''rich'' could easily ignore such attacks as religious reformers might mount on their behaviour. These attacks were insignificant in terms of the power structures which the rich monopolised. Pleas for the poor in later Old Testament literature, or in the Roman context, should not be invested with ''political'' significance.

CHAPTER EIGHT

FOURTH CENTURY WATERSHEDS

> "God, seeing himself contemned by our nature, out of his goodness has handed it over to certain princes to correct it... Because of our depravity there was need of government."
>
> St. John Chrysostom, *Sermo in Genesim*, 4, 2.

Examination of the economic problem by the Christian Fathers of Late Antiquity was undertaken in a context which differed substantially from that of their predecessors. After Constantine, the Roman Empire remained nominally pluralistic with respect to religious belief and observance. However, the Emperors (with the notable exception of Julian the Apostate, 360-363) remained committed to the Christian cause and discriminated accordingly. The old aristocratic families, which dominated the senate at Rome, clung to paganism and represented a countervailing political force, at least to the end of the fourth century. This force was of some significance in the Western Empire for a time, but had little or no viability in the East.[1]

Another new factor conditioning the thought of the later Fathers was economic decline. The roots of that decline extend well back beyond the accession of Constantine, and it may be traced to trends that were becoming apparent in the closing decades of the second century.[2] Early Christian Emperors, however, displayed no capacity to reverse those trends, so conditions in many regional economies continued to worsen throughout the fourth and fifth centuries.

A third important element in the foundations of later patristic economic thought was the phenomenon of monasticism. This phenomenon emerged partly as the result of economic deprivation and of an imperial order with which the life of the Church was becoming increasingly identified. Monasticism inspired some of the Fathers to seek for a set of economic relationships other than that which pertained conventionally as part of the fabric of Empire.

---

[1] Consult, Arnaldo Momigliano (ed.), *The Conflict Between Paganism and Christianity in the Fourth Century* (Oxford: Clarendon Press, 1963), pp. 31-33.

[2] See, e.g., Arthur E. R. Boak, *Manpower Shortage and the Fall of the Roman Empire in the West* (Ann Arbor: University of Michigan Press, 1955), p. 19.

CHRISTIAN RESPONSIBILITY

Constantine's adoption of Christianity presented the Church with a range of issues which it had not been obliged to meet previously. As Arnold Jones has remarked: "It was difficult for Christians to adjust their ideas when under Constantine, the government became Christian ... The Church had never had to face the moral problems of a Christian placed in a position of secular authority, and on some very elementary points it was still in doubt almost a century after Constantine's conversion."[3] Some Christians were now in a position to exercise social responsibility on an unprecedented scale. They could tread the corridors of power and shape the future of the society within which they had been merely a reactive group hitherto.

What was the model for action on the political plane? Here, the *New Testament* appeared to offer little that encouraged a positive response to the new opportunity. "It has always been difficult," writes Elizabeth Isichei, "to extract any unequivocal political doctrine from the recorded sayings of Jesus ... For this reason, the political attitudes of later Christians were very largely determined by the views of Paul, whose injunction to the Romans to be subject to the 'powers that be' was probably the most influential pronouncement in the history of political thought."[4] Further, political action for social reform was discouraged by the view that government was a matter for the *imperium*, and obedience to its directives was mandatory. Geza Alfoldy states: "Disobedience to the ruler was regarded not only as a criminal act but as sacrilege ... the emperor, even on the Christian view, was the chosen one to who *summa divinitas* transferred the government of all things on earth."[5]

The idea that Christians might take responsibility for the fate of the Empire was also diffused by a certain euphoria surrounding Constantine's conversion. Among the Fathers, Eusebius of Caesarea (265-337) was prominent in the expression of that euphoria. For Eusebius, "the kingdom and empire of Constantine is resplendent as an image of the kingdom of heaven."[6] It has been contended that Eusebius' view of

---

[3] A. H. M. Jones, *The Later Roman Empire, 284-602* Vol. 2 (Oxford: Blackwell, 1964), p. 983.

[4] E. A. Isichei, *Political Thinking and Social Experience: some Christian interpretations of the Roman Empire from Tertullian to Salvian* (Christchurch: University of Canterbury Publications, No. 6, 1964), p. 21. C. F., Wilfred Parsons, "The Influence of Romans XIII on Pre-Augustinian Christian Political Thought", *Theological Studies*, 1 (1940), pp. 337-364.

[5] G. Alfoldy, *The Social History of Rome* (London: Croom Helm, 1985), p. 188.

[6] F. Edward Cranz, "De Civitate Dei, XV, 2, and Augustine's Idea of the Christian Society," *Speculum*, 25 (1950), p. 220. See also, Theodor E. Mommsen, "St. Augustine and the Christian Idea of Progress," *Journal of the History of Ideas*, 12 (1951), p. 362.

Christian kingship was typical of the fathers of the fourth and fifth centuries.[7]

Almost certainly, Eusebius' view was not typical. Even the Greek Fathers, "consistently rejected caesaropapism. The emperor was admonished many times that his *imperium* did not comprehend 'the things of God.'"[8] Further, for the majority of the Fathers, the existing political order was not an image of the Kingdom but rather, a necessary evil that must be tolerated as an alternative to social chaos.[9] Nevertheless, the Fathers did not doubt that an emperor had authority from God and that the authority included regulation of the economic life of the Empire as he chose.

Each of the foregoing considerations contributed to the puzzle of what form effective Christian social action might take on anything but the basis of a local faith-community (the traditional, pre-Constantinian basis). The puzzle was further compounded in the case of intervention in economic affairs. In the first place, economic studies had no place in the Roman intellectual tradition.[10] Secondly, there was nothing (or, almost nothing) in the political life of the Empire that could be termed "economic policy". Arnold Jones writes:

> "I do not believe that it [the Roman government] had any economic policy, save in a very rudimentary sense. The Roman government was interested in the revenue, and in acquiring precious metals and the mines which produced them, but in very little else in the economic sphere."[11]

No doubt, within a few decades of Constantine's accession the Church had become an outstanding factor in public life, especially in the East.[12] Also, there is little doubt that the Church, "attracted the most creative minds ... almost all born rulers, rulers of a type which, with the exception of the scholarly emperor Julian, it was hard to find on the imperial throne."[13] Yet these creative and, in some instances, powerful figures were unable to translate their commitment to social responsibility into action for reform of the Roman economy from within. The combination

---

[7] Francis Dvornik, *Early Christian and Byzantine Political Philosophy* (Washington: Dumbarton Oaks Center for Byzantine Studies, 1966) Vol. 2, pp. 681-699.

[8] Michael Azkoul, "Sacerdotium et Imperium: the Constantinian Renovatio according to the Greek Fathers," *Theological Studies*, 32 (1971), p. 452.

[9] C.f., Kenneth M. Setton, *Christian Attitudes Towards the Emperor in the Fourth Century* (New York: Columbia University Press, 1941), pp. 193-194.

[10] Charles Norris Cochrane, *Christianity and Classical Culture* (New York: Oxford University Press, 1957), p. 149.

[11] A. H. M. Jones, *The Roman Economy* (Oxford: Blackwell, 1974), p. 137.

[12] Cf., Hans von Campenhausen, *The Fathers of the Greek Church* (London: Black, 1963), p. 84.

[13] A. Momigliano, op. cit., p. 9.

of factors outlined above proved too great an obstacle. As the church rose in the affairs of Empire, the problem of scarcity continued to press ever more keenly on large sections of the populace.

ECONOMIC DECLINE

The progressive deterioration of the regional economies of the Empire forms a consistent background to the economic thought of the later Fathers. Underlying that deterioration was a conjunction of factors which constituted a powerful prescription for negative growth. Those factors included: capital starvation; lack of innovation; population decline; and, decreasing mobility of labour. The incidence of the conditions for declining productivity was enhanced by a failure of government to adjust its demand for revenue to the diminishing taxable capacity of the Empire. Further, those conditions were exacerbated by a marked trend to increasing concentration of ownership in the agricultural sector, which sector was by far the most predominant in virtually all of the regional economies. This trend could well have been crucial in ensuring that economic decline meant economic stagnation. Its importance has been emphasised by Arnold Jones, who writes: "If I may venture a generalisation on the economic effects of the Roman Empire I would say that its chief effect was to promote an ever increasing concentration of land in the hands of its governing aristocracy at the expense of the population at large."[14]

Capital starvation was nothing new in the Empire. Even in its economic hey-day the system does not warrant the appellation "capitalistic".[15] A better term is "acquisitive". Moses Finley points out that, "the strong drive to acquire wealth was not translated into a drive to create capital; stated differently, the prevailing mentality was acquisitive but not productive."[16] Citizens who acquired capital used it mainly for conspicuous consumption or to purchase land, domestic slaves, and houses. The economic growth phase of the Empire is not attributable to an upsurge of capitalistic behaviour. Rather, it turned on the establishment of law and order over an expanding territory. This permitted wider and more stable trading arrangements, greater security of property, and urbanisation which facilitated exploitation of the advantages of the division of labour.[17] This environment certainly encouraged

---

[14] A. H. M. Jones, op. cit., p. 135.
[15] C. N. Cochrane, op. cit., p. 141.
[16] M. I. Finley, *The Ancient Economy* (London: Chatto and Windus, 1973), p. 144.
[17] C.f., Muriel F. Lloyd Prichard, "The Roman Contribution to Economic Growth", *Prudentia*, 2 (1970), pp. 1-5.

capitalistic activity and investment in support of productive labour, but this activity and the investment were not at the centre of the growth process.

In the late Empire, it would appear, capitalism was pushed even further to the periphery of economic life, at the same time as the factors which had made for the initial growth were losing their potency. A major turning point was provided by the fiscal and administrative changes introduced by the Emperor Diocletian (284-305) and upheld subsequently by his Christian successors. Under the new system, so Cochrane observes, "the former paradise of the bourgeoisie was converted into a veritable hell on earth. As Lactantius graphically put it, it was equally expensive to live and die."[18] A wide range of Draconian measures aimed at ensuring an ample and assured flow of money, goods, and services to support central government served to greatly restrict the scope for private entreprise, and to render returns on enterprise uncertain. This meant that, "land was almost the only safe and permanent form of investment, and successful professional men and merchants and craftsmen, who wished to provide for their old age and for their families, did so by buying land."[19]

Existing and potential capitalists, it should be noted, were not only prone to become landowners. There was also a strong incentive to reject a career in business for that of a bureaucrat. The Diocletian reforms had encouraged the growth of massive civilian and military bureaucracies, and the upwardly mobile took advantage of the opportunities these presented. Ramsay MacMullen writes that, under the Christian emperors:

> "The means of bettering oneself had changed, less often through private enterprise, more often through government service, whether armed or civilian; the middle rung of the ladder, the bourgeoisie as a whole, had almost vanished; but class barriers were by no means insurmountable."[20]

Probably, there were considerable opportunities for social mobility in the fourth century, but they do not seem to have been conducive to economic enterprise. In all likelihood, their availability reduced the volume of

---

[18] C. N. Cochrane, op. cit., p. 175.

[19] A. H. M. Jones, *The Later Roman Empire, 284-602* Vol. 2 (Oxford: Blackwell, 1964), p. 772. See also, Keith Hopkins, "Elite Mobility in the Roman Empire", *Past and Present*, 32 (1965), p. 12.

[20] R. MacMullen, "Social Mobility and the Theodosian Code", *Journal of Roman Studies*, 54 (1964), p. 50. See also, K. Hopkins, op.cit., p. 23. Arthur Boak (op. cit., p. 101) comments: "... the civil service became more and more a highly desired haven of refuge for those who sought to escape from the hopelessness of the hereditary careers of the curiales, corporati, and coloni."

capital which might have been expended in support of productive labour and reduced the volume of new capital which might have been created.

As in the case of capital starvation, lack of innovation in productive processes was nothing new in terms of the economic history of the Empire. The dominant sector, agriculture, was notoriously stagnant in the matter of technical procedures. Arnold Jones observes that, "Palladius, who wrote an agricultural manual in the fourth century, lays down the same rules as had Columella in the first."[21] However, it would appear that in the late Empire, agriculture went into reverse. In particular, previous gains in land-use and management were eroded. Technical procedures might not have worsened, since at this stage they could well have taken on the status of eternal verities. Yet, it is highly likely that there was an erosion of ground attained by earlier initiatives in the non-technical aspects of innovation in agricultural production functions.

In the late Empire, the quality of the managerial imput in agriculture fell markedly. Courtenay Stevens remarks that, "with the growth of large estates, the 'master's eye', the value of which early writers well recognize, was less often seen ... So often was the agricultural producer a slave or serf, that the thinking man, whose thinking life was passed in the towns with townsmen, accepted rather than understood what the peasant was doing."[22] The deterioration in managerial imput begins to be explicable when the character of the structure of ownership of land is taken into account. Increasingly, the ownership of land had become the province of the very rich. Arthur Boak writes:

> "The wealthy aristocracy of the Late Empire was composed of inner circles of the senatorial order. They were the great landholders who furnished the higher officials of the bureaucracy and to some extent the army. Their estates grew as the smaller proprietors were sold out by the government or handed over their properties to their more influential neighbours and became their serfs rather than face the imperial tax collectors."[23]

Such a shift in the structure of ownership does not necessarily imply a deterioration in the quality of management. However, when it is appreciated that the owners had no great incentive to treat their lands as an economic asset, then the reasons for the decline from earlier levels of

---

[21] A. H. M. Jones, op. cit., p. 767.

[22] C. E. Stevens, "Agriculture and Rural Life in the Later Roman Empire", in, M. M. Postan (ed.), *The Cambridge Economic History of Europe*, Vol. 1 (Cambridge: Cambridge University Press, 1966), pp. 104-105.

[23] A. E. R. Boak, op. cit., p. 127. The accumulated wealth of an average senatorial landholder was twenty times greater than that of even the most affluent merchant of Alexandria. See, A. M. H. Jones, *The Roman Economy* (Oxford: Blackwell, 1974), p. 138.

productivity become clearer. Under the Christian emperors, "the rich men of the Empire mostly made their money by booty, governmental exortion and corruption, the profits of government contracting, and to a lesser extent official salaries."[24] Agricultural land was purchased by these men for purposes of prestige and enhancement of political status rather than as a means of deriving income. Gradually, the sector of the Roman economy with which that economy was virtually identical came into the governance of men for whom the returns on the performance of that sector were of marginal interest, at best.[25]

Under these circumstances, it is not surprising that the absentee owners and their managers had little incentive to persist with the cultivation of low-yield land that prior innovations had made available. Post-Diocletian taxation rates diminished the incentive even further. These rates, "reduced the landlord's net rent on marginal land to vanishing point."[26] Small landed proprietors may have been prepared to hold on and try to keep poorer land in cultivation, but they were subject to the same taxation rates as the leviathians of the land. The impossibility of meeting the state's demands drove many of these small proprietors into an exile which left their acres fallow. Courtenay Stevens comments that, "a traveller might find men living in remote deserts 'to escape taxation'; their normal holdings would become derelict, but it might be long before the government accepted that they were."[27]

Apart from lack of venture capital and the abandonment of the cultivation of land, the later Empire was subject to substantial population decrease. There is little doubt that the decrease in rural areas was due to a combination of the growing concentation of ownership of land, and the continuing fiscal demands of central government. "Taxation" writes Arnold Jones, "rose so high as to discourage the cultivation of marginal land and the cultivated area, and with it agricultural production, sank. The peasants, on whom the burden ultimately fell, were left so little of their crops that malnutrition and starvation reduced their numbers."[28] City dwellers were also to decrease. This was due to the fall in effective demand for the goods and services which they supplied to the affluent bureaucrats and absentee landords who constituted their local aristocracies. These latter began to find the government's imposts on

---

[24] ibid., p. 136.

[25] Most aptly, Moses Finley designates land ownership as "a non-occupation" of the wealthy. M. I. Finley, op. cit., p. 109.

[26] A. M. H. Jones, *The Later Roman Empire, 284-602* Vol. 2 (Oxford: Blackwell, 1964), p. 823.

[27] C. E. Stevens, op. cit., p. 115.

[28] A. H. M. Jones, *The Roman Economy* (Oxford: Blackwell, 1974), p. 135. See also, A. H. M. Jones, op. cit., p. 1043.

their time and finances too burdensome whilst they continued to fulfil the customary local civic duties. They responded, "by retiring to their estates, into a condition of maximum self-sufficiency, withdrawing their custom from the industrial producers in the city and adding to the damage already wreaked by the government."[29]

One further element in the prescription for negative growth was the attempt by central government to immobilise labour and capital in the interest of ensuring that its needs would be met on a perpetual basis. That attempt has been summarised by Arthur Boak, as follows:

> "Law after law reiterated the life-long obligation of the individual to his particular class or corporation and its activities, the perpetual lien of the state municipality, or college, upon his property for financing the performance of its functions, the hereditability of his status by his heirs, the ban upon attempts to alter one's inherited condition, and the prohibition to change one's place of residence."[30]

According to the letter of these laws, most types of human factor input were immobilised. Agricultural workers and their children were bound to the land they tended. Craftsmen, and their children, were confined to their particular trades. Workers in the State manufacturing industries were similarly constrained. The *fabricenses* (or, arms manufacturers) were actually branded like slaves to aid detection should they endeavour to find alternate employment. Capital transfer was also tightly controlled. Investments in most lines of production could not be withdrawn for use in other avenues. The property of local town councillors (*curiales*), was assigned in perpetuity to ensure the financing of local government expenditures.

As they stand, the laws represent a set of formidable constraints on economic activity in the non-governmental sector, and they are anything but conducive to individual enterprise. However, it may be that many of them were honoured more in the breach than the observance. Keith Hopkins, for example, argues: "The spate of fourth-century laws against social mobility has traditionally been regarded as evidence of immobility. But the laws were only spasmodically enforced; their repetition is evidence of their failure."[31] Again, Arnold Jones contends that they carried far less weight in the Eastern empire than may have been the case in the West.[32] These demurs may be relevant, but it is clear that the tenor of the laws was against any revival of economic dynamism. The *imperium*

---

[29] M. I. Finley, op. cit., p. 161. See also, G. Alfoldy, op. cit., p. 187.
[30] A. E. R. Boak, op. cit., p. 125.
[31] K. Hopkins, op. cit., p. 13.
[32] A. H. M. Jones, op. cit., pp. 48-49, and, *The Later Roman Empire, 284-602*, Vol. 2 (Oxford: Blackwell, 1964), p. 861.

of the Christian emperors seems to have been intent on destroying the material base of the power to which it clung. In sum, there was, "alienation of Roman society from its state system. Compulsion and centralisation were the only responses that the imperial monarchy could offer to the growing economic difficulties, the social and political problems, and the ideological conflicts of Late Antiquity."[33]

The Monastic Reaction

With respect to the future of Western social thought, by far the most significant Christian reaction to the problems of the later Empire was monasticism. The monastic movement, in its inception, had little or nothing to do with the Christian clerical structures of its day. It was essentially a lay movement.[34] Further, the thoroughgoing asceticism which was central to the way of life it involved seems to have more to do with the *New Testament* record regarding John the Baptist rather than Jesus of Nazareth. Concerning that record, Edward Schillebeeckx has observed:

> "Whereas John's call to conversion was essentially bound up with ascetic, penitential practices, the call of Jesus seems to have a fundamental connection with being a table-companion, eating and drinking together with Jesus, an activity in which Jesus' disciples could legitimately feel that the 'latter-day', that is, crucial and definitive, exercise of God's mercy was already present. To believe in Jesus is to put one's trust gladly in God; that is no occasion for fasting."[35]

It is not surprising then that modern scholars locate the conceptual origins of monasticism in non-Christian Jewish practices mediated by a current of Christian thought which the Church was to find heretical. Timothy Barnes, for example, writes: "The Christian monasticism of the later Roman Empire appears to derive ultimately from first-century Judaism, whose traditions of asceticism preserved in Mesopotamia, may have been reintroduced to Syria, Palestine, and Egypt by Manichean missionaries."[36]

---

[33] G. Alfoldy, op. cit., p. 187. On the decay of Roman civilization in a particular region (North Africa), see, W. H. C. Frend, *The Donatist Church* (Oxford: Clarendon Press, 1971).

[34] G. Florovsky, "Empire and Desert: Antinomies of Christian History", *Greek Orthodox Theological Review*, 3 (1957) p. 148. See also, A. Baker, "Messalianism: the Monastic Heresy", *Monastic Studies*, 10 (1974), p. 139.

[35] E. Schillebeeckx, *Jesus, an Experiment in Christology* (London: Collins, 1979), p. 204. C.f., Herbert Musurillo, "The Problem of Ascetical Fasting in the Greek Patristic Writers," *Traditio*, 12 (1956), pp. 45-47. See also, Rudolph Arbesmann, "Fasting and Prophecy in Pagan and Christian Antiquity," *Traditio*, 7 (1949-51), p. 32.

[36] T. D. Barnes, *The New Empire of Diocletian and Constantine* (Cambridge, Mass.: Harvard University Press, 1982), p. 195.

The Christian version of monastic asceticism began in Egypt with the anchorite style of Saint Anthony (250-356). These hermits solved the economic problem at a personal level by rigorous restriction of consumption requirements and by engaging in seasonal agricultural employment at harvest time.[37] Later, Saint Pachomus pioneered a communal framework for the ascetic life, establishing a type of monastery at Tabennesis in 307. The communities founded in the wake of this innovation adopted an orderly approach to caring for their own, modest needs and for those of the poor in nearby areas. "The Pachomian monasteries," according to Jones, "were highly organised industrial and agricultural concerns. The monks worked in gangs under foremen at a great variety of trades, as smiths, carpenters, tailors, fullers, tanners, shoemakers, basketmakers, copyists, as well as at agricultural work. The surplus products were sold in the market, and the money devoted to charity."[38]

Both the anchorite and communal models of asceticism flourished in their desert settings. Each model was economic-rational in its own way and offered a meaningful alternative to life within the Empire. For the early anchorities, in particular, there was sanctuary from Diocletian's wholesale persecution of Christians, which began in 303. The alternate life-styles also offered a measure of freedom for the dispossessed. Arnold Ehrhardt states:

> "There can be no doubt that the immense popularity of monasticism in the East, since the second half of the third century, had its one great cause in the intolerable economic burden which the secular life put on the shoulders of those unfortunate 'villeins' of the early Byzantine Empire."[39]

Not only the persecuted and exploited found the desert communities attractive alternatives. There were also those who could not accept a Christianity that was part of a political establishment. Every religion includes a proportion of persons who think they must be killed or, at least, suffer extraordinary physical deprivation to be true to their beliefs, and early Christians were no exception. When the Empire became nominally Christian and the threat of death was no longer on offer, desert asceticism was a tempting substitute. "The nature of Christian devotion," as Timothy Barnes observes, "inevitably changed when the constant threat of persecution diminished and then disappeared. Asceticism replaced martyrdom as the highest ideal to which Christians could nor-

---

[37] A. H. M. Jones, *The Later Roman Empire, 184-602*, Vol. 2 (Oxford: Blackwell, 1964), p. 792.

[38] ibid., p. 931.

[39] A. Ehrhardt, *The Framework of the New Testament Stories* (Manchester: Manchester University Press, 1964), p. 308.

mally aspire.''[40] In addition to those seeking self-imposed deprivation, there were others for whom monasticism offered the hope of the emergence of a new social order free of the horrors of the post-Contantine regimes. These latter, ''had no trust in the 'christened Empire'. They rather distrusted the whole scheme altogether. They were leaving the earthly Kingdom, as much as it might have been actually 'christened', in order to build the true Kingdom of Christ in the new land of promise, 'outside the gates', in the Desert.''[41]

Born out of a variety of social circumstances, and a combination of understandings and misunderstandings of what it meant to be a follower of Jesus, monasticism put the final seal on paganism in the Greco-Roman milieu. The old beliefs and rituals were emptied of content. Peter Brown writes: ''The stance of the monks was a crushing rebuke to the religious style of the pagan world. A studied rejection of the usual manner of weilding power in society from supernatural sources completed the process of 'anachoresis'.''[42] Beyond this, early monasticism threw out a challenge of major dimensions to the existing social order:

> ''The monks were not helping the Empire to survive. Judged from the traditional point of view of the pagan society they were a subversive force. But they provided an alternative to pagan city life. Monasticism is the most obvious example of the way in which Christianity built something of its own which undermined the military and political structure of the Roman empire.''[43]

This development had a profound impact on the thinking of some of the later Fathers, and it was the work of Basil the Great, in particular, to bring the new social model out of the Desert into co-existence with the day-to-day life of the Empire. One consequence of this work was the emergence of a new perspective concerning ''society'' and ''state''. The new perspective gained ground with intellectuals in the West as well as the East, and it challenged not only Roman but also pre-Christian Greek understandings. Hence, R. A. Markus comments:

> ''If for Aristotle a society which was not political was meaningless, it was not so for Augustine and the Christian fathers... From their [the fathers']

---

[40] T. D. Barnes, op. cit., p. 194.
[41] G. Florovsky, op. cit., p. 146.
[42] P. Brown, *The Making of Late Antiquity* (Cambridge, Mass.: Harvard University Press, 1978), p. 93.
[43] A. Momigliano, op. cit., p. 12. C.f., Paul J. Fedwick, *The Church and the Charisma of Leadership in Basil of Caesarea* (Toronto: Pontifical Institute of Mediaeval Studies, 1979), p. 40.

point of view, 'social' and 'political' were by no means synonymous con-
cepts, as they had to be for Aristotle.''[44]

Another consequence of the formation of the monastic model was the
stimulation of new thinking concerning economic relationships. For the
Fathers, there was no good reason why the vast mass of their fellow
citizens should remain permanently committed to a condition of grinding
poverty. In particular, the monastic milieu demonstrated that economic
relationships could be established on a viable basis without the presence
of the acquisitive mentality which, as was remarked above, dominated
the conduct of the economic life of the Empire. In fact, the Fathers
believed that mentality to be at the root of the problem of scarcity which
pressed so severely on the bulk of the populace.

---

[44] R. A. Markus, ''Two Conceptions of Political Authority: Augustine, De Civitate
Dei, xix, 14-15, and some Thirteenth-Century Interpretations'', *Journal of Theological
Studies*, 17 (1965), p. 92.

CHAPTER NINE

CHARITY AND COMMUNISM

> "For if each one, after having taken from his wealth whatever would satisfy his personal needs, left what was superfluous to him who lacks every necessity, there would be neither rich nor poor."
>
> St. Basil the Great, *In Illud Lucae*

> "The dwellers in the monasteries live just as the faithful did then [i.e., in Jerusalem]: now did ever any of these die of hunger? Was ever any of them not provided for with plenty of everything? Now it seems, people are more afraid of this than of falling into a boundless bottomless deep."
>
> St. John Chrysostom, *In Acta*

Economic decline, the increasing identification of Christianity with Empire, and the emergence of monasticism eventually combined to produce new approaches to the solution of the economic problem. One of these was the Solution by Charity, a systematically argued case for the extension of the practice of local Christian communities since apostolic days to general application in the wider society. This Solution is identified, especially, with Saint Basil the Great (330-379), a scion of the regional aristocracy of Cappadocia. Closely associated with Basil's thought is that of his younger brother, Saint Gregory of Nyssa (335-394), and of Basil's friend, Saint Gregory of Nazianzus (330-390).

A slightly younger contemporary of the Cappadocian Fathers, Saint John Chrysostom (344-407), was also a proponent of the same Solution. However, Chrysostom, who taught in Antioch and became Bishop of Constantinople, came to regard this Solution as a "second-best". He put forward a type of Solution by Communism. Chrysostom's view was influenced by what he understood to be the practice of the primitive Christian community in Jerusalem (see, Chapter Seven). Even more influential was the example afforded by the revolution which St. Basil had achieved within monasticism. Concerning that revolution, Louis Bouyer writes:

> "It would be difficult to imagine a more radical change in any institution than that effected by Basil with monasticism. As he wished it to be, it is almost the exact opposite of what it had been to begin with. From an essentially solitary effort towards liberation; it became, quite the contrary, an essentially communitarian institution."[1]

---

[1] L. Bouyer, *The Spirituality of the New Testament and the Fathers* (New York: Seabury Press, 1963), p. 340.

Basil brought coenobitical monasticism out of the Desert and into the Empire. Chrysostom was so impressed by this communitarian way that he urged its adoption as the pattern for the organisation of economic relationships in society in general.

THE BOUNTY OF CREATION

The starting point for the Greek Fathers' approach to the problem of scarcity is the proposition that the Creator is benevolent. In their view: "God loves man (*philanthropos*), is the divine Distributor (*oikonomos*) of good things, the universal Lord (*pantokrator*), the Friend and Protector of man, from whose care none is excluded. His kindness embraces the whole man."[2] Further, God not only gives resources abundantly, he gives them to mankind in common. Hence, Chrysostom writes:

> "The world is meant to be like a household, wherein all the servants receive equal allowances, for all men are equal, since they are brothers."[3]

The biblical basis for the Fathers' position is found in the *Book of Genesis*. The relevant passage reads: "And God blessed them, and God said to them, 'Be fruitful and multiply, and fill the earth and subdue it; and have dominion over the fish of the sea and over the birds of the air and over every living thing that moves upon the earth. And God said, 'Behold I have given you every plant yielding seed which is upon the face of all the earth, and every tree with seed in its fruit; you shall have them for food. And to every beast of the earth, and to every bird of the air, and to everything that creeps on the earth, everything that has the breath of life, I have given every green plant for food." (Gen. 1:28-30).

Nature, then, is usually bountiful rather than niggardly. Basil assures his readers that: "He who provided pasture for horses and cattle, thought of your riches and pleasure ... He who feeds your cattle, will provide for all the needs of your life."[4] Gregory of Nyssa makes the same point in terms of hospitality and the idea of the world as God's house. In Gregory's treatment, "... God, the perfect Host, having prepared everything, ushers man his guest into the world."[5]

---

[2] E. Trimiadis, "Christian love for strangers according to the early Fathers", *Diakonia*, 9 (1974), p. 234.

[3] Chrysostom, *On II Cor, xii.*

[4] Basil, *Hexameron*, V, 40D. On Basil and the philanthrophy of God, see, D. J. Constantelos, *Byzantine Philanthropy and Social Welfare* (New Brunswick, N.J.: Rutgers University Press, 1968), pp. 33-36.

[5] R. A. Greer, "Hospitality in the First Five Centuries of the Church", *Monastic Studies*, 10 (1974), p. 48. See also, Walter Shewring, *Rich and Poor in Christian Tradition* (London: Burns Oates and Washbourne, 1948), p. 65.

A major problem for those who, like Basil, wish to assert the bounty of creation is the recurrence of natural disasters. Basil's general answer to this problem is to treat such disasters as providential. They are means whereby God punishes and educates mankind. A case in point is the devastating Cappadocian drought of 368. Margaret Mary Fox observes:

> "There was also a great drought in 368 A.D. of which Saint Basil gives a graphic description ... 'What is the cause of this disorder and confusion in nature? What is this strange novelty of the seasons?', Saint Basil asks. And his answer? God's justice on a sinful, neglecting people. Thus he saw in this unusual year the Hand of God, chastening the people for their sins and for their neglect of Him."[6]

The argument from providence was also employed to explain another issue engendered by affirmation of the bounty of creation. That issue is the lack of disposition of natural resources on a uniform geographical basis. The Fathers contended that the non-uniformity was providential, and this involved them in strong support for inter-regional trade, especially sea-trade, as an integral part of God's plan. The Fathers were not imprisoned in the notion that any part of the Empire (Palestine included) was a "promised land", so they were able to look to wider horizons than most of the authors of the Old Testament.

Basil, for one, was a great enthusiast for trade. He argues that trade, "supplies the merchant with his wealth, provides the necessities of life, allows the rich to export superfluities, and blesses the poor with a supply of what they lack."[7] John Chrysostom expounds at length on this theme:

> "For in order that the length of journeying might not be a hindrance to mutual communion, God laid down the sea as a shorter route all over the earth, in order that dwelling as it were in the world as in one house, we should thus frequently visit others and that each should easily share with his neighbours what he had, and receiving from them, even though he occupied a small portion of the earth, he would be the master of all, and should enjoy the good things existing everywhere, exactly as if it were possible to each one of those feasting at a rich table to give what was placed beside him to him as reclined at a distance, and to receive in return that which lay beside the other by merely stretching out the hand."[8]

This panegyric on the God-given character of trade represents an extraordinarily expansive antique view of what is involved in the contest with scarcity, but it must be appreciated that Chrysostom had the advan-

---

[6] M. M. Fox, *The Life and Times of St. Basil the Great as Revealed in His Works* (Washington: Catholic University of America Press, 1939), p. 7.
[7] ibid., p. 19. Consult, Basil, *Hexameron*, IV, 39C.
[8] Chrysostom, *De Compuctione ad Stelechium*, II, 5.

tage of viewing the economic problem from the perspective of Antioch.[9] Waiting in the little rural backwater of Nazianzus, Gregory was able to share some of Chrysostom's regard for God's intention in a diverse disposition of resources.[10] However, he was not prepared to allow that sea-trade was a universal answer to economic difficulties. Gregory argues that,

> "Maritime cities easily endure such privations [i.e., famine] without difficulty, as they give what they have, and receive what comes by sea. But for us of the continent [i.e., residents of Nazianzus] both the surplus was not to be bought, nor can we prepare by any art those things which we lack and we could neither dispose of anything we had, nor bring in anything which was lacking."[11]

Gregory's demur clearly reflects the problems of any small rural community in any age as compared with those of large urban conglomerates where the division of labour can be exploited. However, his demur also points up one of the intractable economic problems of the Empire, namely, the high cost of land transport.[12] As Peter Brown states: "We shall never understand the life of the towns of the Greco-Roman world unless we re-live, through the texts, the creeping fear of famine. However we may draw our maps of the grandiose road-system of the Roman world, each small town knew that they would have to face out alone a winter of starvation, if ever their harvest failed."[13]

THE CAUSES OF SCARCITY

Since resources are almost always readily available to meet the needs of mankind, there is no necessary barrier to the production of commodities in sufficient volume to meet those needs. Hence, scarcity, if it is a general problem, must be engendered by behaviour relating to consumption and distribution. Such behaviour can be modified, if men have the will. Therefore, scarcity is a man-made phenomenon.

In any society, the rich create the problem of scarcity for themselves by continually expanding their consumption horizons, and by anxiously

---

[9] For the background to Chrysostom's perspective, see, J. H. W. G. Liebeschuetz, *Antioch, City and Imperial Administration in the Later Roman Empire* (Oxford: Clarendon Press, 1972).

[10] Gregory of Nazianzus, *Oratio*, 28, 27.

[11] Gregory of Nazianzus, *Oratio* 43. *In Laudem Basilii Magni*, 34.

[12] A. H. M. Jones, *The Roman Economy* (Oxford: Blackwell, 1974), p. 37. See also, the same author's, "Industry, Trade, and Transport", in his, *The Later Roman Empire, 284-602*, Vol. 2 (Oxford: Blackwell, 1964), p. 824ff.

[13] P. Brown, *Religion and Society in the Age of Saint Augustine* (London: Faber, 1972), p. 15.

hoarding wealth against the threat of future need. The poor, by contrast, have the problem thrust upon them by institutionalised economic inequality. The foundations of the pressure of scarcity, as experienced by the poor, are: the existence of the institution of private property; the covetousness of mankind; and, the disproportionate direction of work-effort to satisfying the demands of the rich for luxuries.

Basil, a wealthy aristocrat, is an accurate observer of the psychology of his own social class. Basil describes the manner in which his class subjects itself to scarcity, as follows:

> "You say you are poor, and I agree with you; for anyone who needs a great many things is poor, and you have a great many needs because your desires are many and insatiable... When they ought to rejoice and give thanks that they are wealthier than so many others, they are troubled and sad because some one is richer than they. When they have equalled his wealth at once they try to reach the fortune of one still richer. When they attain a wealth equal to his, they transfer this emulation to a third."[14]

Basil, like Karl Marx, also remarks on the peculiar lack of attachment to personal use-values of his contemporary rentier-capitalists. The Cappadocian Father adds: "When will you use what you have acquired at present? When will you enjoy it, since you are always constrained by the toil of making new acquisitions?"[15]

Similar observations on the self-subjugation of the rich are found in the writings of other Fathers. They also distinguish the factors which subjugate the poor. One of these factors is the institution of private property. This institution, the Fathers found "unnatural", and they had strong grounds for this finding in both pagan and Judeo-Christian tradition. M. J. Wilkes writes: "Of the many strains of classical thought inherited by the Fathers one of the more unexpected was the Stoic tradition of the natural community of property; and this was found to accord well with the Biblical accounts of the communal system put into operation by the early Christian community at Jerusalem."[16] Further, they interpreted the *Book of Genesis* as portraying an "original" common bestowal of ownership of resources.[17]

Covetousness was a second, and favourite, ground for explaining the position of the poor. Chrysostom, for example, in a typical rhetorical flourish, declared that, "did everyone look on gold as so much straw, evil would have disappeared from the world long ago."[18]

---

[14] Basil the Great, *In Divites*, 56C-57B.
[15] ibid.
[16] M. J. Wilkes, "The Problem of Private Ownership in Patristic Thought and an Augustinian Solution of the Fourteenth Century", *Studia Patristica*, 6 (1962), p. 531.
[17] See, e.g., Gregory of Nazianzus, *Or.*, 14, 26, and 32, 22.
[18] Chrysostom, *On Matthew*, xlvi, 4.

A third ground was the misallocation of labour to satisfy the ephemeral requirements of the well-to-do. Basil the Great is of particular interest on this theme, as he employs the same kinds of distinctions concerning occupations as were to be emphasised subsequently by Adam Smith. Like Smith, Basil asserts the primacy of agricultural activity.[19] Again, Smith's criterion for distinguishing productive from unproductive labour is exactly anticipated in Basil's remarks on "the arts". According to Basil, dancing and music have no object but themselves, whereas in the creative arts the work lasts after the operation. These latter include the activities of the brass worker, the architect and the weaver. Basil and Smith are both anxious to promote such activities, where the work lasts *after* the operation.[20]

THE SOLUTION BY CHARITY

The rich, as we have seen, can solve their problem of scarcity by purely personal means. It is a matter of limiting their consumption horizons and, especially, eschewing attempts to emulate the consumption patterns of those who are wealthier. However, the poor do not have such options. To meet the predicament of the poor, the Fathers urge radical charity on the part of the rich, particularly on the part of the rentiers. For Chrysostom, charity was the supreme virtue, ranking well ahead of such ascetical favourites as celibacy and fasting.[21] For Basil, charity was *the* answer to the incidence of scarcity. He wrote: "For if each one, after having taken from his wealth whatever would satisfy his personal needs, left what was superfluous to him who lacks every necessity, there would be neither rich nor poor."[22]

This Solution by Charity was in direct accord with the stewardship theory of property rights that was common to the Fathers. The theory was expressed by Chrysostom, for example, as follows:

> "For you are steward of your own possessions, not less than he who dispenses the alms of the church. As then he has not a right to squander at random and at hazard the things given by you for the poor, since they

---

[19] Basil, *Reg. fus. Interr.*, 38, 384E-385C. Other recommended activities are cobbling, carpentry, architecture, and blacksmithing.

[20] Basil, *Hexameron*, 1, 7c.

[21] C.f., H. Musurillo, "The Problem of Ascetical Fasting in the Greek Patristic Writers", *Traditio*, 12 (1956), pp. 8-9. This is also true for Augustine. See, e.g., S. J. Grabowski, "The Role of Charity in the Mystical Body of Christ according to Saint Augustine", *Revue Des Etudes Augustiniennes*, 3 (1957), pp. 29-63.

[22] Basil, *In Illud Lucae*, 49D. Radical charity was revolutionary in terms of pagan practice. See, M. I. Finley, *The Ancient Economy* (London: Chatto and Windus, 1973), p. 39; and, D. J. Constantelos, op.cit., pp. 11-12.

were given for the maintenance of the poor; even so neither may you squander your own. For even though you have received an inheritance from your father, and have in this way all you possess: even thus, all are God's."[23]

Further, the Fathers contended that while the poor will benefit in material terms, the rich will benefit spiritually from the Solution. Basil was prepared to argue that charity to the poor is absolutely essential for ensuring personal salvation.[24] Much less common is the macro-economic argument for charity. However, it is put forward by Basil, as follows: "As a great river flows by a thousand channels through fertile country so let your wealth run through many conduits to the homes of the poor. Wells that are drawn from flow the better; left unused, they go foul. So money kept standing still is worthless; moving and changing hands, it helps the community and brings increase."[25] This passage is sometimes interpreted as a call to rentiers to engage in productive investments.[26] Given the character of the late Roman economy and the perceptions of the Fathers, it is much more likely to be simply a call for charitable giving.

A variety of questions is raised by the Solution by Charity, and some of them are considered by the Fathers. The questions include, how much should be given by the rich; and the general answer is, all above the ordinary needs of life. This answer gives rise to a further question as to whether or not those "ordinary needs" can be understood as varying from person to person. Chrysostom, for one, is ready to allow variability. He writes:

> "Let him that can be satisfied with pulse and can keep in good health, seek for nothing more; but let him who is weaker than this and requires to be dieted with garden herbs, not be hindered of this. But if any be even weaker than this and require the support of flesh in moderation, we will not debar him from this either. For we do not advise these things to kill and injure men but to cut off what is superfluous; and that is superfluous which is more than we need."[27]

Yet another relevant question is whether or not the charitable giving should be discriminate or indiscriminate. As Donald Attwater recognises, Chrysostom seems to be in favour of indiscriminate giving.[28]

---

[23] Chrysostom, *In Matthaeum*, 74, 4.

[24] Basil, *Hom. in Divites*, 4.

[25] Basil, *In Illud Dictum Evangelii*, 3.

[26] See, e.g., Demetrios J. Constantelos, "Basil the Great's Social Thought and Involvement", *Greek Orthodox Theological Review*, 26 (1981), p. 84.

[27] Chrysostom, *In Epistolam II ad Corinthios*, 19, 3.

[28] Donald Attwater, *St. John Chrysostom, Pastor and Preacher* (London: Harvill Press, 1959), p. 67.

Certainly, he has no respect for scruples as to whether a poor person is "deserving" or "undeserving", and he attacks those those wish to discriminate on such grounds.[29] However, Basil takes a different view. He cites, "with approbation a saying of a certain Heraclides than one should distinguish between needy and greedy begging. Whosoever, he continued, gives to necessity, gives to God, and will receive reward; he who gives to every beggar, throws to a dog, bothersome on account of his impudence, but not to be pitied on account of his need."[30]

The Solution by Charity also poses the issue of the extent to which, if at all, the rich should liquidate assets—lands, houses, and slaves—to facilitate their alms-giving. There is total ambiguity on this issue, such that it is difficult to ascribe any clear, general position even to any one writer. With respect to slave-capital, it is understandable that the Fathers would be reluctant to recommend that Christian masters put their slaves on the open market where they may be purchased by owners who were not constrained by the "household codes" enunciated in the New Testament epistles. Further, it can be observed that in the case of at least two of the Fathers, they would have been against the sale of slaves on the grounds that the correct course of action was emancipation, not liquidation. In his fourth homily on *Ecclesiastes*, St. Gregory of Nyssa takes the extraordinary step, in terms of tradition and contemporary thought, of arguing that slavery is wrong in principle. As John Maxwell has observed, Gregory, "provides the first truly 'anti-slavery' text of the patristic age. As events turned out, his argument against the very institution whereby one man owns another did not bear fruit for another 1,400 years."[31]

The other Father to come out against slavery was John Chrysostom. Flying in the face of all established mores, Saint John recommended that Christians should provide an education in a craft for their slaves, and then emancipate them. This so shocked the congregation to which he was preaching at the time that he was obliged to break off with the comment: "But, I see that I am making you angry".[32]

---

[29] Chrysostom, *De Lazaro*, Concio II, 5, 6. See also his, *De Eleemosyna*, 6, and, *In Hebraeos*, 11, 4.

[30] Joseph B. Hubbard, *Economic Thought in Patristic Literature* (unpublished Ph. D. thesis, Harvard University, 1923), pp. 228-229. The relevant passage is in Basil's, *Epistola*, 150, 3.

[31] John Francis Maxwell, *Slavery and the Catholic Church* (Chichester and London: Barry Rose Publishers, 1975), pp. 32-3.

[32] D. Attwater, op.cit., p. 70. The relevant sermon is Chrysostom's *On I Corinthians*, 40, 6. M. I. Finley, op.cit., p. 88, claims the ancient Christian writers never called for the abolition of slavery. This claim is patently incorrect. The correct observation is that such calls are rare in the surviving literature.

On land and houses, the strong impression is that the Fathers did not carry their Solution by Charity to the extent of urging the rentiers to sell these assets. All of the Fathers are trenchant in their attacks on the land-owners of their era, but these attacks are directed at the landowners' obsession with conspicuous consumption (the *persona* factor), and at the trend to growing concentration of ownership and control of land which marked the Empire in decline.

Even Chrysostom, child of a very sophisticated urban environment (Antioch), and no "country gentleman" with land and slaves like St. Basil, does not require the disposal of assets as part of his "second best" Solution. Hence, at one point Chrysostom remonstrates:

> "I am often reproved for always attacking the rich. Of course I do, for they are always attacking the poor—and anyhow, I never attack the rich as such but only those who misuse their wealth. I keep on pointing out that I accuse not the rich but the rapacious: wealth is one thing, covetousness quite another. Learn to distinguish things and not to confuse together what ought not to be confused."[33]

Chrysostom and Communism

As remarked above, the Solution by Charity was a "second-best" for Chrysostom. His most-preferred solution was by way of communal ownership of property. The Saint of Antioch and Constantinople argued that if his urban congregations were to achieve the type of life envisaged for them by Jesus Christ, they had to rid themselves of the notion that what they had in their possession was somehow an extension of them-selves, and thereby, exclusive of others. Further, if they were to act in terms of freedom of this notion, the community as a whole would benefit greatly.

Chrysostom contends that private ownership breeds conflict in any society.[34] The social model to be emulated is that of the Christian com-munity in Jerusalem, as reported in the New Testament.[35] Chrysostom paints a romantic (and, biblically inaccurate) picture of the economic life of the Jerusalem community, where he claims, "that by selling their

---

[33] Chrysostom, *On the Fall of Eutropius*, 2, 3. It should be noted that St. John's "rich" were of much the same ilk as those of St. Basil and the other Cappadocians. Liebeschuetz writes that, "the aristocracy of Antioch was not a commercial aristocracy... [it was] a class whose chief wealth came from the estates that its members owned and from the func-tions of government that they performed." (J. H. W. G. Liebeschuetz, op. cit., p. 49.)

[34] Chrysostom, *In Epistolam I ad Timotheum*, 12, 4.

[35] Chrysostom, *In Acta*, 11, 3.

possessions they did not come to be in need.''[36] In this same sermon he
goes on to affirm that communism is cheaper—"it is the living separately
that is expensive and causes poverty"—and that monastic experience
demonstrates the viability of what he is proposing in terms of the problem
of scarcity:

> "The dwellers in the monasteries live just as the faithful did then: now did
> ever any of these die of hunger? Was ever any of them not provided for with
> plenty of everything? Now it seems, people are more afraid of this than of
> falling into a boundless bottomless deep. But if we had made actual trial
> of this, then indeed we should boldly venture upon this plan. What grace
> too, think you, would there not be!... What Gentile would be left? For my
> part, I think there would not be one; we should so attract all, and draw
> them to us. But yet if we do but make a fair progress, I trust in God that
> even this shall be realized. Only do as I say, and let us successfully achieve
> things in their regular order; if God grant life, I trust that we shall soon
> bring you over to this way of life."[37]

Chrysostom's most-preferred Solution did not impress the congregations
to which he preached. In addition, it does not seem to have impressed
contemporaries among the Fathers. Even within the confines of patristic
thought, there were ready objections to hand. It could be claimed, for
example, that inequality of wealth was providential. Such inequality
implied the existence of necessitous poverty, and the presence of the poor
provided the rich with the opportunity to attain salvation through
charitable acts. Furthermore, necessitous poverty was conducive to
salvation for the poor. Their condition obliged them to work, and this
obligation freed them from the temptations of idleness. St. John himself
was no stranger to this latter line of reasoning. Leisure, he argued,
encouraged evil-doing.[38] He even essayed a macro-economic case for the
providential nature of poverty:

> "For if with a fitting knowledge and with well considered reflection, you
> were willing to examine this point too, even if there were nothing else which

---

[36] Not only Chrysostom, but the Fathers in general, must be accounted often wildly
inaccurate commentators on the Bible. J. Duncan M. Derrett observes: "When we turn
to the fathers we see some astonishing things, and we search amongst them for traces of
genuine tradition. Pathetically, alarmingly few, they do testify to a feeble continuity with
Jewish thought. The present writer would urge as an undertaking the systematic attempt
to list all traces, however feeble, of the church's hold upon the tradition of the apostles
in the matter of Christ's individual teachings." J. D. M. Derrett, "The Parable of the
Prodigal Son: Patristic Allegories and Jewish Midrashim", *Studia Patristica*, X, 1 (1970),
p. 222.

[37] Chrysostom, ibid.

[38] Chrysostom, *In Illud: Salutate*, 1, 5. See also, *In Epistolam I ad Corinthios*, 5, 4. St.
John also expounded on the spiritual benefits to the rich of alms-giving. Consult, *In
Titum*, 6, 2.

confirms the providence of God, riches and poverty would evince this most clearly. For if you take away poverty you would take away the whole basis of life, and you would destroy our [manner] of life, neither will there be sailor, nor pilot, nor farmer, nor mason, nor weaver, nor shoemaker... nor any other of these workers; and if these did not exist, all things would perish for us. For now like the best kind of mistress, the compulsion of poverty sits on each of these, and drives them to work even against their will.''[39]

In sum, it would seem that Chrysostom never reconciled his adherence to the Solution by Charity with his advocacy of communism. Further, he failed to spell out the organisational details of his new communistic order beyond references to the Jerusalem community and the contemporary example of the monks. As Joseph Hubbard has concluded:

"Chrysostom, in the spirit of a reformer, brought forward a proposal for the reorganization of the life of the Christians, which was confessedly radical, but which he regarded as an attainable ideal. For this proposal he advanced ordinary communistic arguments of the cheapness of common living, the removal of inequality, and the abolition of poverty ... He hardly gave consideration to the economic aspect of his plan, nor did he face squarely the question of the continuation of charitable acts after its adoption.''[40]

Chrysostom's final position with respect to the economic problem was that of Utopian Communism. Yet, his approach cannot be dismissed as entirely utopian, in that it was inspired, in large measure, by the tangible, practical example of monasticism. Such was St. John's attachment to the monastic model as a spiritual and social ideal that, ''in his opinion, separate monasteries should exist now, in order that one day the whole world might become like a monastery.''[41] The monks, he thought, had established the correct pattern of Christian living, and it was time that this pattern was adopted in the cities of the Empire.

---

[39] Chrysostom, *De Anna*, 5, 3.
[40] J. Hubbard, op.cit., p. 216.
[41] G. Florovsky, ''Empire and Desert: Antinomies of Christian History'', *Greek Orthodox Theological Review*, 3 (1957), p. 149. C.f., Gerhart B. Ladner, *The Idea of Reform: its impact on Christian thought and action in the age of the Fathers* (Cambridge, Mass.: Harvard University Press, 1959), pp. 126-127.

CHAPTER TEN

STOICISM AND AGRICULTURE

> "God did not make the sea to be sailed over, but for the sake
> of the beauty of the element... The sea is given to supply you
> with fish to eat, not for you to endanger yourself upon it; use
> it for purposes of food, not for purposes of commerce."
>
> St. Ambrose of Milan, *De Elia*

Saint Ambrose of Milan (339-397) left an indelible mark on socio-economic thought in the West. His Christian beliefs were combined with a great reverence for certain of the old Roman traditions, and he was able to offer a viable Western counterpart to the social thought that was emenating from the Fathers of the East. Through the centuries, aspects of Ambrose's work have provided influential conduits through which the ideas of some pre-Christian thinkers, notably Cicero (106-44 B.C.), have flowed on into the mainstream of European Christianity. Homes Dudden writes that,

> "it is owing to his (Ambrose's) natural affinity with Stoicism that so much
> of the old Stoic morality became incorporated, first, in his own treatise,
> then through that treatise in the ethics of the Middle Ages, and finally in
> the common thought of Christendom at the present day."[1]

The impact of the "treatise" in question, namely, *De officiis ministrorum* has been remarked by Edwin Hatch who observes that Ambrose's book, "is a *rechauffee* of the book which Cicero had compiled more than three centuries before, chiefly from Panaetius. It is Stoical, not only in conception, but also in detail... The ethics of the Sermon on the Mount, which the earliest Christian communities endeavoured to carry into practice, have been transmuted by the slow alchemy of history into the ethics of Roman law. The basis of Christian society is not Christian but Roman and Stoical."[2] Nevertheless, the book should not be construed as radical in its day, as many Christian communities in the West were already well

---

[1] F. Homes Dudden, *The Life and Times of St. Ambrose*, Vol. 2 (Oxford: Clarendon Press, 1935), p. 551.

[2] Edwin Hatch, *The Influence of Greek Ideas on Christianity* (New York: Harper, 1957), p. 169. C.f., A. H. Armstrong and R. A. Markus, *Christian Faith and Greek Philosophy* (London: Darton, Longman and Tood, 1960), p. 102; and, M. L. W. Laistner, *Christianity and Pagan Culture in the Later Roman Empire* (Ithaca: Cornell University Press, 1951), p. 64.

on the way to acceptance of pagan ethics as their own.[3] *De officiis* and other of Ambrose's writings serve to define, at least as much as they determine the future of, Latin Christianity.

COMMON OWNERSHIP

Despite his celebrated interventions in the realm of church-state relationships, Ambrose is a conservative figure in the history of Western social thought. Hence, it is surprising that he can be associated with the idea of a revolution in the economic order as fundamental as that envisaged by St. John Chrysostom. Homes Dudden, for example, contends that, "Ambrose denies altogether the right to own private property. He holds that private property is contrary alike to the ordinance of God and the law of Nature, and is a deplorable abuse originating in human avarice."[4] This contention can be grounded in a variety of statements by Ambrose. In the *De officiis* he writes:

> "Nature has poured forth all things for the common use of all men. And God has ordained that all things should be produced that there might be food in common for all, and that the earth should be the common possession of all. Nature created common rights, but usurpation has transformed them into private rights."[5]

Ambrose returns to the same theme on other occasions. "God meant this earth," he affirms, "to be the common possession of all men and to produce its fruits for all, but avarice has created the various rights of property."[6] Again, he challenges his readers: "Why do you think that any portion of the world is common to all? And why do you reckon that the fruits of the earth are private, when the earth itself is the property of all in common?"[7]

Passages such as these suggest that for Ambrose, the only truly Christian economic order is one based on the principle of common possession. Yet, in practice, he does not recommend such an order. Louis Swift points out that Ambrose, "not only argues that wealth can be an incentive to virtue (in Luc 5.69; 8.85; epist. 2.11; in psalm 40.31) and that giving up all one's possessions in pursuit of Christian perfection is a mat-

---

[3] See, Henry Chadwick, *Early Christian Thought and the Classical Tradition* (Oxford: Clarendon Press, 1966), p. 5: and, Hans Dieter Betz (ed.), *Plutarch's Ethical Writings and Early Christian Literature* (Leiden: Brill, 1978), p. 8.

[4] F. Homes Dudden, op.cit., p. 545.

[5] Ambrose, *De officiis*, i, 132.

[6] Ambrose, *Expos. ps. XCVIII*, 8, 22.

[7] Ambrose, *De Viduis*, 5.

ter of spiritual counsel rather than obligation (vid. 12.73; off. 1.30.149),
but he holds property himself, he allows his clergy to do so, and he even
gives them advice on how they might best use their wealth to serve the
needs of others.''[8]

The fact that Ambrose is able to affirm a communistic ideal but to treat
that ideal as practically irrelevant is thoroughly consistent with his Stoic
background. According to the Stoics, the institution of private property
is not "natural", but it is justified as an evil which should be tolerated
in the contemporary state of mankind. For Cicero as for Seneca,
"neither a right to private property nor coercive political regimes can
appeal to the sanctions of any supposed prototype in nature or primitive
society. Yet ... these two conventions are henceforth indispensible, serving as they do to hold in check or to remedy still greater wrongs."[9]
Ambrose's position is also consistent with the Judeo-Christian tradition
concerning a radical change in social relationships related to the Fall of
Man. For Ambrose, "*iustitia* is an equivocal term when applied to man
before and after Original Sin. Before the Fall it involved the kind of
altruism that was incompatible with private property ... Subsequent to
the Fall, however, both the altruistic character of the virtue and the
absolute prohibition against property it involved became relative."[10]

It is incorrect, then, to associate Ambrose with Chrysostom as an
advocate of communism as the best Christian response to dealing with
the problem of scarcity. Rather, Ambrose's approach is akin to that of
Clement of Alexandria (see, Chapter Seven). Any meaningful solution
to the scarcity issue turns on the use, not the disposition of ownership,
of property. As Swift has observed:

> "One of the most revealing statements about the new [i.e., post-Fall] rela-
> tionship between possessions and public responsibility is Ambrose's remark
> in *in psalm* 118.8.22 ... Private property need not be relinquished, but its
> benefits, its *usufructus*, must be shared ... proper *usus* makes private property
> compatible with *iustitia* in man's present state."[11]

The close relationship of Clement and Ambrose on this issue is not surprising. The social theories of both were based on blends of New Testament and Stoic understandings.[12]

---

    [8] Louis J. Swift, "Iustitia and Ius Privatum: Ambrose on Private Property", *American
Journal of Philology*, 100 (1979), p. 185.
    [9] D. J. MacQueen, "St. Augustine's Concept of Property Ownership", *Recherches
Augustiniennes*, 8 (1972), p. 199.
    [10] L. J. Swift, loc. cit.
    [11] ibid., pp. 185-186.
    [12] On Clement and Stoicism, see, H. Chadwick, op.cit., p. 42.

COMMERCE ASSAILED

In marked contrast with the Greek, Clement, the Latin, Ambrose has little or no time for commercial activity. His position on the question is strongly reminiscent of that of Tertullian (see, Chapter Seven). Homes Dudden writes that, "commerce in general is condemned by Ambrose. His attitude is partly accounted for by the fact that he does not appear to recognize the possibility of honest trade. In his mind commerce is associated with false weights, short measures, fraudulent agreements, and contracts, and every species of dishonesty... quite apart from any question of deliberate fraud, Ambrose reprobates commerce on the following grounds—that it distracts a man's thoughts from virtue and fixes them on money-making, that it encourages him to be artful and cunning, that it substitutes the ruthless struggle of business competition for fraternal rivalry in friendly offices."[13]

There are many examples in his writings of Ambrose's antipathy to commercial activity. One of the most peculiar of these is an attack on sea-trade.[14] He is also amongst the most vehement and comprehensive of patristic writers in the condemnation of usury.[15] Typically, he augments the standard biblical quotations against usury with Cato's assertion (reported by Cicero) that lending to someone at interest is the equivalent of killing that person.[16] This theme of interest-taking as a form of homicide is carried over by Ambrose into a curious justification of the practice, under some conditions. Those Fathers who wished to eliminate interest-taking in any shape or form had special difficulties with the Old Testament allowance that the people of God could lend at interest to foreigners.[17] Ambrose, uniquely, deals with these difficulties by recourse to the doctrine of just war. Ambrose asks:

> "Who is then the foreigner unless Amalec, unless Amorrhaeus, unless an enemy? There, it says, exact usury, whom you justly desire to kill, against whom arms are justly borne, for him usury is justly appointed. Whom you cannot easily conquer in war upon him you can quickly avenge yourself by *centesima* [charging interest at one per cent per month]. From him exact usury, whom it would not be a crime to kill. Without the steel he is

---

[13] F. Homes Dudden, op.cit., pp. 548-549.

[14] Ambrose, *De Elia*, 70, 71. A somewhat more friendly assessment of maritime commerce is offered in his *Hexaemaron*, iii, 22.

[15] Consult, R. P. Maloney, "The Teaching of the Fathers on Usury", *Vigilae Christianne*, 27 (1973), pp. 250-255.

[16] Ambrose, *De officiis*, ii, 25, 89.

[17] For discussion of the allowance, see, B. Gordon, "Lending at Interest: some Jewish, Greek, and Christian Approaches, 800 B.C.—A.D. 100", *History of Political Economy*, 14 (1982), pp. 409-412.

diminished, who suffers usury: without the sword he who becomes the exacter of usury from the hostile avenges himself upon the enemy. Therefore, where there is justice in war, there also is justice in usury.''[18]

Except in the foregoing context, Ambrose condemns not only interest on loans to consumers, but also on loans to businessmen employing the capital for commercial purposes. The interest cannot be taken in the form of either goods or money. He writes: ''And since many, avoiding the precepts of the law, when they would give money to businessmen, do not exact usuries in money, but collect returns in merchandise; therefore let them hear what the law says: Thou shalt not receive from your brother interest of victuals, it says, nor of anything which is lent upon interest.''[19] Here, Ambrose's objection appears to turn on the implicit assumption that businessmen are pricemakers operating on a cost-plus basis. Because they are obliged to pay interest, the businessmen will inflate the prices of their products.[20] Ambrose continues: ''And do you [the lender] think to do justly, when you receive as it were a present from the businessman? Thence he commits fraud in the price of goods, whence he pays you usury. Of this fraud you are the author, you the sharer, for yours is the profit from whatever he does in fraud.''[21] The Saint of Milan does not consider, or even to seem to recognise the existence of, the case where a businessman is a price-taker operating in a market subject to competition.

In accord with his thoroughly jaundiced view of the world of commerce, Ambrose finds no justifiable role for accumulation as an activity. From the viewpoint of any individual person, it is a foolish pursuit.[22] Like his Eastern contemporary, Basil of Cappadocia (see, Chapter Nine), Ambrose observes how the rich can impose the problem of scarcity on themselves. Ambrose asks:

> ''Do you suppose that he possesses riches, who, brooding over his treasure night and day, is tormented by covetousness and wretched anxiety? Nay, such a one is in want. Although he appears rich to others, to himself he is poor, because, while he is ever grabbing and desiring more, he does not use that which he has. Where there are no bounds to covetousness, what profit can there be in riches?''[23]

Yet, riches do not automatically entail damnation. This depends on the way in which accumulated wealth is used: ''Not all poor men are blessed

---

[18] Ambrose, *De Tobia*, 15, 51.

[19] ibid., 14, 49.

[20] C.f. J. B. Hubbard, *Economic Thought in Patristic Literature* (unpublished Ph.D. thesis, Harvard University, 1923), p. 191.

[21] Ambrose, loc. cit.

[22] See, e.g., Ambrose, *De officiis*, i, 241-244.

[23] Ambrose, *Ep.* 38.6.

for poverty is a neutral state; there can be bad poor as well as good. Not all who possess riches are condemned by the Divine judgement, but those who know not how to use them.''[24]

AGRICULTURE AND CHARITY

In the sphere of politics, Ambrose can be portrayed as an innovator in that he sought to put limits on the authority of the Emperor with respect to issues that could be regarded as essentially religious in character. Further, in his view, there were ethical norms to which the Emperor should be subject in secular matters.[25] Nevertheless, Ambrose was anything but a revolutionary. He was deeply nostalgic for republican Rome but saw no viable alternative to the emperors. In fact, in the opinion of Francis Dvornik, he was, ''optimistic and considered that republican perfection could be achieved under a wise monarchy, provided both monarch and subjects understood their duties. Only anarchy could succeed the destruction of monarchy...''[26]

In the sphere of economics, Ambrose was profoundly conservative (even, reactionary), as his attitude towards commercial activities demonstrates. Legitimate economic pursuits were agricultural pursuits, and legitimate command of wealth was based on inherited land. Ambrose, ''has all the old Roman respect for a landed estate inherited from one's fore-fathers. Such a property is almost a part of the family, and to dispose of it lightly or to sell it for money seems to him a kind of sacrilege (see, *De officiis*, ii, 17; iii, 63; *De Nabuthe*, 13). On the other hand, to cultivate, improve, and extract profit from such an estate is not only legitimate but praiseworthy.''[27]

A Christian working inherited land can be free from Ambrose's strictures with respect to accumulation. He has not come into possession of the land by way of covetousness. Further, agricultural activity is the case *par excellence* in which private property is employed to benefit the community at large as well as the owner of that property. Agriculture, ''alone affords men an opportunity of enriching themselves without injuring their neighbours; at the same time it improves the earth, fosters the virtues of industry, patience, foresight, and thrift, and rewards the worker in strict proportion to the thought and energy he has expended (see, *De*

---

[24] Ambrose, *Expos. ev. Luc. VIII*, v. 53, 69.
[25] C.f., Kenneth M. Setton, *Christian Attitudes Towards the Emperor in the Fourth Century* (New York: Columbia University Press, 1941), pp. 213-215.
[26] F. Dvornik, *Early Christian and Byzantine Political Philosophy* (Washington: Dumbarton Oaks Center for Byzantine Studies, 1966), Vol. 2, p. 676.
[27] F. Homes Dudden, op.cit., p. 549.

officiis, iii, 38-40).''[28] In rural pursuits, fallen mankind can approximate something of the altruism which pertained before the Fall.

As well as devotion to agriculture, a Christian economic order requires devotion to charity by the rich. Like the other Fathers, Ambrose concentrates on the idea that the rich must be prepared to give generously to those in need if they are to have any hope of personal salvation. However, at one point, he also employs a macro-economic argument for almsgiving. Ambrose writes:

> "How unprofitable for their city that so large a number should perish, who were wont to be helpful either in paying contributions or in carrying on business. Another's hunger is profitable to no man, nor to put off the day of help as long as possible and to do nothing to check the want. Nay more, when so many of the cultivators of the soil are gone, when so many labourers are dying, the corn supplies will fail for the future."[29]

With respect to the dispensation of charity, Ambrose recommends an approach which does not discriminate between the "deserving" and "undeserving" poor.[30] Nevertheless, he draws a line with respect to aid for itinerants who have made a profession of begging.[31]

Ambrose's Christian society incorporates the traditional institution of slavery. The Saint preached radical charity, but not the emancipation of slaves. To justify the continuation of slavery, Ambrose employed the Stoic argument that a person who is wise and good is free, whatever that person's legal status. He also argued that it was probably better for weak characters to be slaves, and that the condition of slavery was conducive to the development of certain personal virtues.[32] The aristocratic Ambrose was too much a man of his social class and era to be able to abstract from a milieu in which, as Arnold Jones comments: "Aristocratic hermits and monks who kept only a slave or two to look after them were praised for their self-denial."[33] Perhaps, there was also an economic base for Ambrose's position. The use of slave labour was an integral feature of the traditional agricultural order which he recommended. Yet, it could be inappropriate to make too much of any economic consideration. This is especially so if it is the case that, "by the fourth and fifth centuries of our era, chattal slavery had lost its key place

---

[28] ibid., p. 550.

[29] Ambrose, *De officiis*, iii, 7.

[30] Ambrose, *De Nabuthe*, viii, 40.

[31] Ambrose, *De officiis*, ii, 15, 73.

[32] Consult, F. Homes Dudden op.cit., pp. 544-545. An excellent survey of the Fathers on slavery is, John Francis Maxwell, *Slavery and the Catholic Church* (Chichester and London: Barry Rose publishers, 1975), pp. 30-44.

[33] A. H. M. Jones, *The Later Roman Empire, 284-602* Vol. 2 (Oxford: Blackwell, 1964), p. 851.

even in the old classical heartland, in the productive urban activity to free labour (independent for the most part), in the countryside to tied tenants known as *coloni*."[34] Further, in the late Empire, the distinction between freemen and slaves became increasingly blurred within the rural workforce.[35]

Situating Ambrose

St. Ambrose is a particularly important figure in the history of the evolution of church-state relations in the West. In 385, for example, he defied the Empress Justina on the question of Arian influence. In 390, he took the Emperor Theodosius to task for the massacre of thousands in Thessalonika, and the emperor underwent public penance in acknowledgement of his guilt. However, as a political theorist, he is not especially innovative. His thought, in this respect, is largely in the Eusebian mould. "On the providential role of the Empire for the diffusion of the Christian faith," writes Dvornick, "Ambrose becomes very eloquent."[36]

As a social theorist, he is greatly indebted to pagan traditions, especially that of the Stoics. Ambrose's disdain for commercial activities for example, is in direct accord with the rating of those activities as mean, vulgar and sordid by Cicero and Seneca.[37] Yet, he succeeds in infusing Stoic ethics with an entirely new dimension deriving from the New Testament. As Homes Dudden states:

> "Stoic charity was little more than refined egoism or self-love—a sort of supreme elegance adorning virtue... Christian charity, on the other hand, effaces itself, puts everyone else before itself. And it is this virtue, unknown to Stoicism, of supreme self-giving, that is accorded the central, overwhelmingly predominant, place in Ambrose's system. This alone is sufficient to impart to his ethics a colouring totally different from that of Stoicism."[38]

The presence of this new dimension is illustrated plainly in the contrast between Ambrose and the classical stoics on the question of alms-giving. Cicero and Sencea urge discrimination and caution in the distribution of alms.[39] Ambrose, on the other hand, recommends a much less discriminatory approach (see, above).

[34] M. I. Finley, *The Ancient Economy* (London: Chatto and Windus, 1973), p. 85.
[35] C.f., J. H. W. Liebeschuetz, *Antioch, City and Imperial Administration in the Later Roman Empire* (Oxford: Clarendon Press, 1972), p. 147.
[36] F. Dvornik, op.cit., p. 681.
[37] Cicero, *De officiis*, 1, 150; Seneca, *Ep.* 88, 21-23.
[38] F. Homes Dudden, op.cit., p. 553.
[39] Cicero, *De officiis*, 1, 42ff; Seneca, *Dial. VII, de vita* 24, 1-3.

In terms of the history of ideas, the bulk of the modern interest in Ambrose turns around the relationship of his thought to that of Augustine of Hippo. At the age of thirty, Augustine moved to Milan to teach rhetoric there. Three years later, in 387, he became a Christian and was baptized by St. Ambrose. Some scholars affirm that significant aspects of Augustine's writings are attributable to Ambrose's influence.[40] What is more certain is, that those ideas of Ambrose's which Augustine found compatible with his own were thereby given an extraordinary lease of life. R. A. Markus comments:

> "...the history of early Christian ethics would be greviously incomplete if the ethical teaching of St. Ambrose were omitted: his re-interpretation in a Christian setting of Ciceronian ethics, largely Stoic in inspiration, was certainly a very great achievement. But through his brilliant convert, Augustine, much that was of most lasting value in Ambrose's synthesis, passed into the generally accepted moral currency of Western Christendom."[41]

On specific matters relating to economic behaviour and organisation, there are a number of obvious, close affinities between Ambrose and Augustine. For example, both emphasise the central role played by charity in a Christian economic order.[42] Again, there is little to choose between the two on the subject of usury. Maloney notes that Augustine's condemnations of the practice do not add notably to the reasonings of Ambrose and the earlier Fathers.[43] Further, like Ambrose, Augustine is prepared to tolerate, and even justify, the institution of slavery.[44]

Despite these affinities, however, there are profound differences between the two Fathers in their understanding of a general, Christian approach to solution of the economic problem. The differences stem from a massive change of perspective concerning the context in which such an approach can be conceived. After Augustine, a solution in terms of the old verities of Empire, however admirable those verities, becomes obsolete. Ambrose's world is obliged to give way to the uncertainties of a people on pilgrimage.

---

[40] See, e.g., F. L. Rozsaly, "Hellenic Elements in the Dialogues of Augustine", *Classical Bulletin*, 32 (1956), p. 31; and, M. L. W. Laistner, op. cit., p. 70.

[41] A. H. Armstrong and R. A. Markus, op.cit., pp. 102-103.

[42] On Augustine, in this regard, see, T. M. Garrett, "St. Augustine and the Nature of Society", *The New Scholasticism*, 30 (1956), p. 26; and, S. J. Grabowski, "The Role of Charity in the Mystical Body of Christ according to Saint Augustine", *Revue Des Etudes Augustiniennes*, 3 (1957), p. 29.

[43] R. P. Maloney, op.cit., pp. 259-261. The same author reports that Augustine, when a bishop, presided over church councils which endeavoured to outlaw usury of any kind. See, R. P. Maloney, "Early Conciliar Legislation on Usury", *Recherches De Theologie Ancienne et Medievale*, 39 (1972), pp. 151-152.

[44] Consult, J. F. Maxwell, loc. cit.; see also, R. A. Markus, "Two Conceptions of Political Authority", *Journal of Theological Studies*, 17 (1965), pp. 71-73.

CHAPTER ELEVEN

ON PILGRIMAGE WITH AUGUSTINE

> "Use the world, let not the world hold you captive. You are
> passing on the journey you have begun; you have come,
> again to depart, not to abide. You are passing on your
> journey, and this life is but a wayside inn. Use money as the
> traveller at an inn uses table, cup, pitcher, and couch, with
> the purpose not of remaining, but of leaving them behind."
> St. Augustine of Hippo, *In Joann. Evangel.*, XL, 10.

New dimensions of socio-economic thought emerge in the West with the
advent of Augustine (354-430). Those dimensions are due, in part, to an
important retrospective element in his writings. "The thought of
Augustine," writes Elizabeth Isichei, "represents a return, partly under
the impact of disaster, to the eschatological values of Jesus, and the early
church."[1] In particular, Augustine begins to recapture a sense of the
Solution by Seeking the Kingdom which Jesus had expounded (see,
Chapter Five). Augustine's Christians are not basically members of time-
honoured households of an Empire that must endure. Rather, they are
pilgrims who are on the road. That road has its foundations in the
realities of time and history, but its direction is not established by any
one set of political and social arrangements, even that of the Roman
Empire. Augustine tries to situate himself and his fellows by employment
of the concept of "the City of God", and, as Barr remarks:

> "Saint Augustine places a great deal of emphasis on the 'pilgrim' character
> of the City of God. A captive on earth, imperfect and not yet solidly estab-
> lished, the City fares through time in the spirit of hope, looking for the
> kingdom of eternity and keeping her heart ever set upon her heavenly
> home."[2]

Apart from this return to Jesus' understanding of the position of Christians in society, Augustine's social thought is also differentiated from that
of most of his patristic forerunners by a more emphatic appreciation of
the relevance to it of the doctrine of the Trinity. That doctrine, by virtue
of the need to defend it against various heresies, had come to be recog-

---

[1] E. A. Isichei, *Political Thinking and Social Experience* (Christchurch: University of
Canterbury Publications: No. 6, 1964), p. 72.
[2] R. B. Barr, "The Two Cities in Saint Augustine", *Laval Theologique et Philosophique*,
18 (1962), 219. C.f., F. Edward Cranz, "Kingdom and Polity in Eusebius of Caesarea",
Harvard Theological Review, 45 (1952), p. 65.

nized as the keystone in the structure of orthodox Christian belief. Augustine expounded the doctrine, and, "implicit in Augustine's whole treatment of the Trinity is an idea of the three persons as the ultimate in the just, equal, common society. Man is summoned, both individually and socially, to realise his created capacity of reflecting this ultimate divine reality by living out, individually and socially, justice and equality and community."[3]

SOCIETY, THE STATE, AND PROPERTY

Augustine defines a people as, "an assemblage of reasonable beings bound together by a common agreement as to the object of their love."[4] For him, there is no doubt that civil society, and the family, are natural to man. However, this latter is not the case with respect to political arrangements. Markus observes, "that after c.400 Augustine continued to think with Cicero, that man was a social animal by nature, but that he came to reject the view that he was also naturally a political animal."[5] Markus continues that the state, according to Augustine,

> "originated in sin, and its purpose was both punitive and remedial. Political authority and its coercive agencies exist for the purpose of coping with the consequences of man's sin, with the disorganization and conflict endemic in the human condition; to prevent men from devouring each other like fish, in Irenaeus's graphic image [*Adv. haer* V, 24, 2]. The sphere of the state is social order, security, material needs; the state is not a means of salvation."[6]

This view, it should be emphasised, is in marked contrast with that of Eusebius of Caesarea.[7] Further, it was a view which probably gained little currency in the East. In the West, as Dvornik observes, Augustine's writings (in contrast with those of Ambrose of Milan) served to, "enlighten his age on the fallacy of identifying the church of the Kingdom of God with the Roman Empire ... But the East did not experience the same disillusionment. It continued in blissful ignorance to identify Church and Empire under the aegis of the emperor as the

---

[3] E. Hill, "Trinitarian Politics: or towards an Augustinian Marxism?", *Prudentia*, 5 (1973), p. 98.

[4] Augustine, *De. civ. Dei*, xix, 24.

[5] R. A. Markus, "Two Conceptions of Political Authority", *Journal of Theological Studies*, 17 (1965), p. 82. C.f. E. A. Isichei, op. cit., pp. 75-76. Consult also, D. X. Burt, "St. Augustine's Evaluation of Civil Society", *Augustinianum*, 3 (1963), pp. 87-94.

[6] R. A. Markus, op. cit., p. 98.

[7] F. Edward Cranz, op.cit., p. 47. See also, the same author's, "*De Civitate Dei*, XV, 2, and Augustine's Idea of the Christian Society", *Speculum*, 25 (1950), pp. 219-220.

representative of God and deputy for Christ."[8] Among the reasons for the greater longevity of this identification in the East was the readier ascendancy there to political power by Christians. Another factor was the lesser attachment, of those who could claim to be educated, to the Roman rhetorical syllabus which continued to point up contrasts between ("refined") paganism and ("uncouth") Christianity. In the West, it was easier to see the difference.[9]

Augustine found that support for the idea of the origin of the state in sin was ready to hand in both biblical and Roman pseudo-history. He was able to contend that political regimes, "have been founded largely through that assertive egoism, that ruthless will to power, which is the hall-mark of the *civitas terrena*. Cain, its archetypal citizen built the first city, and Romulus, like Cain, was a fratricide."[10] Nevertheless, Augustine was too well schooled in Socratic philosophy to condemn any social institution because of its origins. The relevant consideration was its end or purpose. Augustine is no anarchist, and he understands the institutions of government as providential. God sanctions those institutions as means of amelioriating some of the worst social consequences of sin.[11] Augustine, "repeatedly appears as the defender of secular government, in opposition to a monastic-type tradition of rejection, which remained strong in the church of his day, and which was espoused in extreme form by the Donatists."[12]

Given society as natural and the state as an unnatural but providential intervention, Augustine set himself a series of massive conundrums which the vast majority of the earlier thinkers of both Christian and pagan antiquity were able to avoid by simply identifying "society" with "state". The difficulties which Augustine's new dualism provoked are well illustrated by his attempts to come to grips with the problem of the ownership of property, a problem that is fundamental to any approach to recommendations regarding economic relationships in society.

To begin to understand Augustine on property, it is helpful to distinguish two questions: how does one acquire property legitimately?; and, how does one maintain the right to continue to hold property already acquired? Augustine's answer to the first question appears to relate to what is natural to man in civil society. It can be argued that:

---

[8] F. Dvornik, *Early Christian and Byzantine Political Philosophy* (Washington: Dumbarton Oaks Center for Byzantine Studies, 1966), Vol. 2, p. 683.

[9] C.f., A. Momigliano (ed.), *The Conflict Between Paganism and Christianity in the Fourth Century* (Oxford: Clarendon Press, 1963), p. 30.

[10] E. A. Isichei, op. cit., p. 75.

[11] C.f., R. A. Markus, op. cit., p. 77.

[12] E. A. Isichei, op. cit., p. 77.

"Augustine held that the legal right to private property is one of the most important civil rights. Natural law secures the common ownership of property, but it is also the basis of our right to private property. We have a natural right to our fair share of what God has created for all men…"[13] One can acquire property naturally (and, legitimately) through inheritance, gift, just conquest, or commercial activity involving market transfer and trade.[14]

When it comes to the second question, however, natural considerations appear to give way to those deriving from either divine law or human law. Arguing against the Donatists Augustine contends:

> "No man can justly possess earthly goods except in one of two ways; either by Divine law, according to which everything belongs to the just, or by human law, which is the power of kings. You have therefore no right to regard what you possess as personal property, since you are not just."[15]

Augustine expands on "the power of kings" in relation to property, elsewhere. He writes: "It is, however, by human right that someone says, this estate is mine, this house is mine, this servant is mine. Human right, therefore, means the right of the emperors. Why so? Because God has distributed these very rights to mankind through the emperors and kings of this world … It is by rights derived from kings that possessions are enjoyed."[16]

The theme of, "Divine law, according to which everything belongs to the just" is taken up in other of his writings.[17] From these, it emerges that, "since common or public ownership precedes private ownership both in time and in nature, the part being greater than the whole, the licit acquisition and possession of property must always remain conditional upon and subordinate to its just use."[18] By definition, just persons acting in conformity with divine law must be using their property well in social terms. Thereby, they have the right to continue to hold that property. Augustine finds support for this "right use" theory of legitimate ownership in Cicero.[19]

From the foregoing, it is clear that the Emperor has the right to deprive the unjust of their property at any time. His right with respect to the just

---

[13] G. J. M. Pearce, "Augustine's Theory of Property", *Studia Patristica*, 6 (1962), p. 498.

[14] See, Augustine, *Sermo*, 50, 2, 4.

[15] Augustine, *Ep.*, 93, 12, 50.

[16] Augustine, *In Iohan.*, ev. tr. 6, 1, 25-26.

[17] See, especially, Augustine, *Ep.*, 153, 6, 26 (to Macedonius); and, *Sermo*, 50, 2, 4.

[18] D. J. MacQueen, "St. Augustine's Concept of Property Ownership", *Recherches Augustiniennes*, 8 (1972), p. 218. See also, G. J. M. Pearce, op.cit., p. 499.

[19] Cicero, *De re publica*, i, 17.

is by no means as clear. In MacQueen's opinion, Augustine's position is that, "the authority of the prince in the political, economic and social sphere is absolute and final; this principle cannot be challenged, nor with one exception, is there any right of appeal from it ... Only when the supreme ruler contravenes a Divine command, does disobedience become a duty."[20] If this is Augustine's position, then it probably meant that, in practice, Augustine would allow the right of the Emperor to confiscate the property of the just in times of communal emergency such as military invasion or famine. Otherwise, a ruler who was observing God's law would have little excuse for demands on the "right-users" beyond those customary calls by way of taxation and other levies deemed necessary to maintain the viability of the state apparatus.

PRODUCTION AND DISTRIBUTION

Economic behaviour is concerned with the production, distribution, and consumption of property. As his treatment of property rights demonstrates, Augustine regarded the acquisition of property, which involves production, as a feature of the natural order. However, the distribution of property is not part of that order. Distribution was a matter of natural processes before the Fall of Man, but because of man's sin it has become the subject of human law augmented by the divine law of charity revealed in the life and teachings of Jesus. For Augustine, then, there is a sharp distinction between production and distribution, a distinction of a kind which was to be made with equal emphasis some fifteen hundred years later in the economic analysis of the philosopher John Stuart Mill.[21]

Augustine's understanding of the meaning of productive activity is based on the biblical exposition by the Yahwist (see, Chapter One). As for the Old Testament writer, man is created a worker and he works in Paradise. It is a thoroughly natural activity which precedes the Fall.[22] Rudolph Arbesman writes:

> "In the task assigned by God to man in the Garden of Eden: 'to till it, and care for it', Augustine sees the beginning of all cultural activity of the human race in its long history—an activity which is characterized by man's legitimate endeavour to fashion the world that surrounds him by efforts of his own mind and freedom according to his own designs."[23]

---

[20] D. J. MacQueen, op.cit., p. 208.

[21] J. S. Mill, *Principles of Political Economy* (1848).

[22] Augustine, *De Genesi ad litteram*, 8, 8.

[23] R. Arbesmann, "The Attitude of St. Augustine Toward Labor", in, David Newman and Margaret Schatkin (eds.), *The Heritage of the Early Church* (Rome: Pont. Institutum Studiorum Orientalium, 1973), p. 249.

Work, it is acknowledged, acquires the "real cost" aspects of pain and toil after the Fall. Sinful man is torn between the obligation to work and desire for fleeting pleasures.[24] Nevertheless, there is an essential continuity, and Augustine underlines the continuity with the contention that in the course of man's aboriginal calamity, nature did not fall with him. For Augustine, "nature is not arbitrary or capricious in its basic aspect, and its operations are not subject to irrational forces or interventions."[25] In his understanding, "the material world lies under no curse, is afflicted with no stain, no subjection to Satan, is not alienated from God because of man's sin. It shares neither the guilt nor the *poena* of man. It does not groan for liberation; it awaits no redemption, no judgement, no purification."[26]

It follows from this that the presence of the problem of scarcity as part of the human condition cannot be attributed to any cursing of mankind's environment by the Creator. The economic problem is something of man's own devising. Further, if productive activity now entails real cost for the worker, it is not because God has rendered nature niggardly. Augustine's position does not fit well with the episode in Yahwistic primeval history where Yahweh proclaims: "Accursed be the soil because of you. With suffering shall you get your food from it every day of your life." (*Genesis*, 3:17). However, it is entirely compatible with the Yahwist's proclamation of a new world order associated with the Covenant with Noah (see, Chapter One).

On the basis of the idea that productive engagements are natural, and are common to both pre-, and post-Fall, mankind, Augustine adopts an approach to the role of work which is revolutionary in terms of both pagan and Christian antiquity. In particular, Augustine, "championed the real moral value and even genuine nobility of manual work—the very work which the upper and leading classes of ancient pagan society, distinguishing between the life of work and the life of culture, so despised."[27] The Greek Fathers, despite their emphasis on the value of work for monks as a means of preventing temptations in idleness, were

---

[24] Augustine, *De. civ. dei*, 22, 22.

[25] Charles P. Carlson, "The Natural Order and Historical Explanation in St. Augustine's 'City of God' ", *Augustiniana*, 21 (1971), p. 422.

[26] Thomas E. Clarke, "St. Augustine and Cosmic Redemption", *Theological Studies*, 19 (1958), p. 150.

[27] R. Arbesmann, op.cit., p. 248. The same writer (ibid., p. 257) points out that: "Augustine's treatise *De opere monachorum* is the first and only attempt of a patristic author to formulate systematically the sentiments of early Christianity toward manual labor, and to assign to the latter its rightful place in the sphere of man's earthly activity." On the pagan view of work, see, Robert L. Wilken, *The Christians as the Romans Saw Them* (New Haven: Yale University Press, 1984), pp. 35-36.

too heavily conditioned by their pagan educations and surrounds to find nobility in manual work.[28] In the West, the Roman-Stoic disdain for such work was also decisive, with even a Saint Ambrose (see, Chapter Ten).

Augustine distinguishes five motives for productive activity. These are: the need to meet personal wants; enjoyment that can be derived from engagement in work; spiritual merit gained by honest toil; freedom from the temptations of idleness; and, ability to give to the poor.[29] His new approach to such activity is illustrated by the manner in which he sets about classifying the occupations involved. At one point, he identifies occupations which, result in a material product; or, assist God in his operations; or, result in action.[30] The second category here is particularly noteworthy. It includes medicine, agriculture, and navigation, and the designation of these avocations as "assisting God" is a rare patristic suggestion that in and through their daily work men and women might be participating in a Divine plan. "Agriculture", it can be added, embraces the vast bulk of the work force of the Roman Empire.

Unlike the majority of his patristic predecessors, Augustine seems to have also had particular regard for the work-world of craftsmen. A vivid illustration of that regard is his treatment of the attempts of a certain collegium of silversmiths to increase its productivity despite the constraints of imperial edicts restricting the mobility of labour. In this instance, "without any condescension the Christian Bishop analysed labour relationships and referred to processes among artisans—something which the philosophers and even inventors had long since ceased to do because of its commonness."[31]

Augustine is even prepared to give merchants their due. Authors like Tertullian and Ambrose find it difficult to understand how such traders might have any legitimate role in a Christian economic order, but Augustine perceives that a member of this suspect section of society can claim to be a worker. He writes:

> "But a trader said to me, behold I bring indeed from a distant quarter merchandise to these places wherein there are not those things which I have brought, by which means I may gain a living: I ask but as reward for my labour that I may sell dearer than I have bought: for whence can I live,

---

[28] C.f., B. Gordon, *Economic Analysis Before Adam Smith* (London: Macmillan, 1975), pp. 92-93.

[29] For detail, see, R. Arbesmann, op. cit., pp. 250-251.

[30] Augustine, *De Doctrina Christiana*, ii, 30.

[31] E. Booth, "A Marginal Comment of St. Augustine on the Principle of the Division of Labour (de civ. Dei VII, 4)", *Augustinianum*, 17 (1977), p. 255.

when it has been written, 'The worker is worthy of his reward' (*Luke*, 10, 7)?''[32]

When he turns from the natural sphere of production to the political sphere of distribution, Augustine is far less innovative in terms of earlier patristic thought. He did not subscribe to an identification of the Roman Empire with the Kingdom of God (see above), but this did not lead him into any campaign for reform of the existing laws influencing the pattern of distribution.[33] From Augustine's perspective: ''Whether government is good or bad, Christian or pagan is essentially indifferent... From the subject's viewpoint, changes in government are comparatively immaterial, and the reign of Nero is as entitled to obedience as that of Theodosius, unless something sinful is commanded.''[34]

Like his predecessors, Augustine puts major emphasis on charity (the divine law imperative) as the chief means of correcting the inequities of the existing distributive process. For him, Charity is central to Christian morality, and a gift of God which does not originate in man's free will.[35] Further, it, ''is more than the fugitive expression of human good nature; it is a form of justice.''[36] However, he has no desire to see Christians impoverished by their giving, and he allows that the degree to which one gives can be a function of that person's customary standard of living. Concerning the latter, he writes:

> ''Let the rich use what their infirmity has accustomed them to; but let them be sorry, that they are not able to do otherwise. For it would be better for them if they could. If then the poor be not puffed up for his poverty, why shouldst thou for thine infirmity? Use then choice and costly meats, because thou art so accustomed, because thou canst not do otherwise, because if thou dost change thy custom, thou art made ill. I grant thee this, make use of superfluities, but give to the poor necessaries; make use of costly meats, but give to the poor inexpensive food.''[37]

Augustine also counsels rationality and sobriety in the distribution of alms.[38] As for himself, a person with command over ecclesiastical pro-

---

[32] Augustine, *Enarrationes in Psalmos, 70*, sermo, 1, 17. See also, his, *Sermo* 117, 5.

[33] C.f., Gerhart B. Ladner, *The Idea of Reform* (Cambridge, Mass.: Harvard University Press, 1959), p. 463.

[34] E. A. Isichei, op. cit., p. 80.

[35] S. J. Grabowski, ''The Role of Charity in the Mystical Body of Christ according to Saint Augustine'', *Revue Des Etudes Augustiniennes*, 3 (1957), pp. 33-34.

[36] G. J. M. Pearce, op. cit., p. 497. C.f., T. M. Garrett, ''St. Augustine and the Nature of Society'', *The New Scholasticism*, 30 (1956), p. 26.

[37] Augustine, *Sermones*, 61, 12.

[38] Augustine, *Enarrationes in Psalmos*, 102, 12.

perty, he is in the position of a trustee for the poor and must distribute with care from that property according to the degree of need involved.[39]

GROWTH AND DEVELOPMENT

Within the framework of thought on the economic problem in antiquity, the idea that there might be a progression over time to an increasingly satisfactory solution of that problem in communal terms is rare, if not totally absent. It can be argued that this idea was an element in the teachings of the Sophists, and that its presence in Greek thought is reflected in the plays of Aeschylus, Sophocles, and Euripides.[40] However, if the prospect of economic growth and development was viable in Periclean Athens, it died when that city-state lost its autonomy. Its burial was presided over by the Socratic philosophers, and their Cynic, Stoic and Epicurean successors ensured that there would be no early resurrection. Roman intellectuals were innocent of the notion. Any economic development that might be associated with the ascendancy of Rome occurred by accident rather than by public policy or the promptings of social theory.[41]

Patristic writers, even after the accession of Constantine, offer no new perspectives in this respect, despite their access to the Old Testament and its treatment of economic growth in both Yahwistic primeval history and the plans for the revival of Israel by post-exilic prophets. Yet, it can be contended that growth and development are envisaged as possibilities by Augustine.

Certain modern scholars have associated Augustine with the idea of "progress". This association has been vigorously contested by other historians of ideas. Amongst the doubters is Theodor Mommsen who finds that, "In Augustine's opinion then, there is no true 'progress' to be found in the course of human history."[42] Edward Cranz has concluded that in some of his earlier writings, Augustine may have countenanced the possibility of progress, but that his mature position comes down to the proposition that the pattern of history is simply, "the

---

[39] Augustine, *Ep.*, 185, 35. See also, M. J. Wilkes, "The Problem of Private Ownership in Patristic Thought and an Augustinian Solution of the Fourteenth Century", *Studia Patristica*, 6 (1962), p. 540.

[40] See, B. Gordon, op. cit., pp. 10-20. Consult also, the outstanding study, Eric A. Havelock, *The Liberal Temper in Greek Politics* (London: Cape, 1957).

[41] C.f., Muriel F. Lloyd Prichard, "The Roman Contribution to Economic Growth", *Prudentia*, 2 (1970), pp. 1-5.

[42] T. E. Mommsen, "St. Augustine and the Christian Idea of Progress", *Journal of the History of Ideas*, 12 (1951), p. 374.

absolute contrast between the damned and the saved.''[43] In line with
these findings, a more recent survey of the modern controversy by
Christopher Berry is capped by the blunt statement that, "to attribute
'progress' to the fourth century, is, at minimum, uninformative and is
arguably unintelligible and bad history.''[44]

How is it possible that Augustine may have begun to break out of the
static formulae of most of antiquity with respect to the economic
problem? One of the bases for such an escape was Augustine's revision
of the conventional perspective on the shape of human history as con-
sisting of some endless, repetitive round. He rejects the classical Greek
cyclical view of history, and replaces it with a linear model in which conflict accounts for observable change. The linearity is derived from his
biblical perspective. Jewish understanding of history is anything but
cyclical in character, and Augustine thoroughly appreciates this. He
writes that, "Scripture is a history of the past, a prediction of the future
and a delineation of the present.''[45] Change is accounted for in the model
by the conflict between "the city of God" and its terrestial antithesis.
History is the outcome of a dialectic process, as was to be affirmed centuries later by Karl Marx.

For the members of Augustine's "City" there is just as much
possibility for improvement in their economic circumstances as there is
for Marx's slowly emerging "proletariat". However, Augustine is
reasoning in much more sophisticated terms than Marx. In Augustinian
terms, the latter errs by thinking that social engineering can effect an
improvement, whereas the reality is that governmental structures are a
matter of indifference (see, above). Augustine is quite definite on how
socio-economic improvement might be attained. He writes that,

> "a people is an assemblage of reasonable beings bound together by com-
> mon agreement as to the objects of their love... It will be a superior people
> in proportion as it is bound together by higher interests, inferior in propor-
> tion as it is bound together by lower.''[46]

Whether or not there is improvement, does not depend on replacing one
social blue-print for another (as the Socratic philosophers believed) but
on alterations in people's "interests". Augustine puts the full weight of
possibility for growth and development on the individuals who comprise
the society in question. He sets the evolution of those individuals as per-

---

[43] F. Edward Cranz, "The Development of Augustine's Ideas on Society Before the
Donatist Controversy", *Harvard Theological Review*, 47 (1954), p. 284.

[44] C. J. Berry, "On the Meaning of Progress and Providence in the Fourth Century",
Heythrop Journal, 18 (1977), p. 270.

[45] Augustine, *De doctrina Christiana*, iii, 10.

[46] Augustine, *De civ. dei*, xix, 24.

sons at the centre of the historical dynamic. This is a revolutionary treatment of personality in terms of classical conceptions of the individual in relation to society.[47] The treatment remains revolutionary in that there are still social theorists who, like Marx, reason about economic growth and development in terms of "class" or some equivalent abstract.

Given his emphasis on the person, it is entirely misleading to associate Augustine with the idea of inevitable progress in human history. There may be growth and development at times, and there is no necessary reason why society may remain locked in a particular pattern of production and distribution. Nevertheless change for the better is not guaranteed within any given time-frame. Nor, in his view, will any such change prove definitive. True justice (*vera iustitia*) is only established at the end of time when God's kingdom comes. Meanwhile, the justice of any *res publica* (whose citizenry, perforce, is a mixture of members of the heavenly with members of the earthly, city[48]) must remain only an image or an approximation of the truth. There is no "final solution" in time such as a Plato could envisage.

Because productive activity is a natural, pre-Fall human propensity, it is Augustine's understanding that, "mathematics, logic, and natural science, the fine arts and technology, may all become both the beneficiaries of the conversion of man's love and the instruments of that new love of God that rejoices in his whole creation and serves all his creatures."[49] However, mankind is fallen, so that there is no guarantee that in acting in terms of that propensity it will necessarily achieve the types of growth and development which the Creator envisaged when He bestowed the gift of work.

AUGUSTINE'S INITIATIVES

St. Augustine's initiatives in social thought are many, and the foregoing sections of this chapter have touched on only a few. In particular, they remark on the significance of his return to the eschatological values of Jesus, and on his awareness that the doctrine of the Trinity has social implications. Additionally, they underline the importance of his distinc-

---

[47] The significance of Augustine's new concept of personality is discussed in, C. N. Cochrane, *Christianity and Classical Culture* (London: Oxford University Press, 1957), p. 386ff.

[48] "St. Augustine's strong and repeated condemnation of the *civitas terrena* cannot be applied to the State as a political institution in general or to any particular State or political collectivity." R. T. Marshall, *Studies in the Political and Socio-Religious Terminology of the De Civitate Dei* (Washington: Catholic University of America Press, 1952), p. 89.

[49] H. Richard Niebuhr, *Christ and Culture* (New York: Harper, 1951), p. 215.

tion between the state and society, and of his explorations of the problem of the ownership of property.

With respect to the problem of scarcity, Augustine conveys a sense of the Solution by Seeking the Kingdom to a greater degree than any of the early Fathers. Further, his thought is differentiated from that of his predecessors by a firm distinction between distribution and production, which distinction permits him to treat work (in some of its forms, at least) as participation in a Divine plan. He pays attention to the work-world of craftsmen, and finds a legitimate role for merchants in a Christian social order. Augustine's thought may also open up the possibility that economic growth and development can be envisaged as part of such an order. However, this last proposition remains controversial.

BIBLIOGRAPHY

Unless it is indicated otherwise, the texts of the biblical passages quoted in this book are taken from Alexander Jones (ed.), *The Jerusalem Bible* (London: Darton, Longman and Todd, 1966). Passages from the Fathers are attributable to a wide variety of sources. The major on-going series of collections of patristic writings in English translation are: Ancient Christian Writers (Westminister, Md.); Catholic University of America Patristic Studies (Washington); and, The Fathers of the Church (Washington). Valuable earlier series are: A Library of the Fathers of the Holy Catholic Church (Oxford); A Select Library of Nicene and Post Nicene Fathers (New York); Library of Christian Classics (London and Philadelphia); and, The Works of Aurelius Augustinus (Edinburgh).

MODERN STUDIES

Ahlstrom, G. W., *Joel and the Temple Cult of Jerusalem* (Leiden: Brill, 1971).
Albright, W. A., *Yahweh and the Gods of Canaan* (London: Athlone Press, 1968).
Alfoldy, Geza, *The Social History of Rome* (London: Croom Helm, 1985).
Allen, L. C., *The Books of Joel, Obadiah, Jonah and Micah* (London: Hodder and Stoughton, 1976).
Anderson, G. W. (ed.), *Tradition and Interpretation* (Oxford: Clarendon Press, 1979).
Arbesmann, Rudolph, "Fasting and Prophecy in Pagan and Christian Antiquity", *Traditio*, 7 (1949-51), 1-71.
——, "The Attitude of St. Augustine Toward Labor", in, David Newman and Margaret Schatkin (eds.), *The Heritage of the Early Church* (Rome: Pont. Institutum Studiorum Orientalium, 1973), 245-259.
Armstrong, A. H. and R. A. Markus, *Christian Faith and Greek Philosophy* (London: Darton, Longman and Todd, 1960).
Attwater, Donald, *St. John Chrysostom, Pastor and Preacher* (London: Harvill Press, 1959).
Azkoul, Michael, "Sacerdotium et Imperium: the Constantinian Renovatio according to the Greek Fathers", *Theological Studies*, 32 (1971), 431-464.
Baker, A., "What Sort of Bread did Jesus want us to Pray for?", *New Blackfriars*, 54 (1973), 125-129.
——, "Messalianism: the Monastic Heresy", *Monastic Studies*, 10 (1974), 135-141.
Barker, E., *From Alexander to Constantine* (Oxford: Clarendon Press, 1956).
Barnes, Timothy D., *Constantine and Eusebius* (Cambridge, Mass.: Harvard University Press, 1981).
——, *The New Empire of Diocletian and Constantine* (Cambridge, Mass.: Harvard University Press, 1982).
Barr, R. B., "The Two Cities in Saint Augustine", *Laval Theologique et Philosophique*, 18 (1962), 211-229.
Barrett, C. K., *A Commentary on the Epistle to the Romans* (London: Black, 1971).
——, *The Gospel According to St. John* (London: S.P.C.K., 1978).
Barrosse, T., "The Unity of the Two Charities in Greek Patristic Exegesis", *Theological Studies*, 15 (1954), 355-388.
Barth, M., *The Anchor Bible: Ephesians* (New York: Doubleday, 1974).
Beare, F. W., *A Commentary on the Epistle to the Philippians* (London: Black. 1969).

Bell, H. Idris, *Cults and Creeds in Graeco-Roman Egypt* (Liverpool: Liverpool University Press, 1953).

Berry, Christopher, J., "On the Meaning of Progress and Providence in the Fourth Century", *Heythrop Journal*, 18 (1977), 257-270.

Best, Ernest, *A Commentary on the First and Second Epistles to the Thessalonians* (London: Black, 1972).

Betz, Hans Dieter (ed.), *Plutarch's Ethical Writings and Early Christian Literature* (Leiden: Brill, 1978).

Biard, Pierre, "Biblical Teaching on Poverty", *Cross Currents*, 14 (1964), 433-440.

Boak, Arthur E. R., *Manpower Shortage and the Fall of the Roman Empire in the West* (Ann Arbor: University of Michigan Press, 1955).

Booth, E., "A Marginal Comment of St. Augustine on the principle of the Division of Labour (de. civ. Dei VII, 4)," *Augustinianum*, 17 (1977), 249-256.

Borne, E. and F. Henry, *A Philosophy of Work* (London: Sheed and Ward, 1938).

Bouyer, Louis, *The Spirituality of the New Testament and the Fathers* (New York: Seabury Press, 1963).

Breuggemann, Walter, *The Land: Place as Gift, Promise and Challenge in Biblical Faith* (Philadelphia: Fortress, 1977).

Bright, J., *The Anchor Bible: Jeremiah* (New York: Doubleday, 1965).

Brown, Peter, *Religion and Society in the Age of Saint Augustine* (London: Faber, 1972).

——, *The Making of Late Antiquity* (Cambridge, Mass.: Harvard University Press, 1978).

Brown, R. E., "The Pater Noster as an Eschatological Prayer", *Theological Studies*, 22 (1961), 175-208.

——, *The Gospel of St. John and the Johannine Epistles* (Collegeville, Minn.: Liturgical Press, 1965).

Burt, D. X., "St. Augustine's Evaluation of Civil Society", *Augustinianum*, 3 (1963), 87-94.

Campbell, Edward F., *The Anchor Bible: Ruth* (New York: Doubleday, 1975).

Campenhausen, Hans von, *The Fathers of the Greek Church* (London: Black, 1963).

Carlson, C. P., "The Natural Order and Historical Explanation in St. Augustine's 'City of God' ", *Augustiniana*, 21 (1971), 417-447.

Chadwick, Henry, *Early Christian Thought and the Classical Tradition* (Oxford: Clarendon Press, 1966).

Childs, B. S., *Exodus, a Commentary* (London: S.C.M., 1974).

Clarke, Thomas E., "St. Augustine and Cosmic Redemption", *Theological Studies*, 19 (1958), 133-164.

Cochrane, Charles Norris, *Christianity and Classical Culture* (New York: Oxford University Press, 1957).

Constantelos, Demetrios J., *Byzantine Philanthropy and Social Welfare* (New Brunswick, N.J.: Rutgers University Press, 1968).

——, "Basil the Great's Social Thought and Involvement", *Greek Orthodox Theological Review*, 26 (1981), 81-86.

Conzelmann, H., *Jesus* (Philadelphia: Fortress, 1975).

Cranz, F. Edward, "De Civitate Dei, XV, 2, and Augustine's Idea of the Christian Society", *Speculum*, 25 (1950), 215-225.

——, "Kingdom and Polity in Eusebius of Caesarea", *Harvard Theological Review*, 45 (1952), 47-66.

——, "The Development of Augustine's Ideas on Society Before the Donatist Controversy", *Harvard Theological Review*, 47 (1954), 255-316.

Creed, J. M., *The Gospel According to St. Luke* (London: Macmillan, 1965).

Cullman, Oscar, *The Early Church* (London: S.C.M., 1956).

Danielou, Jean, *A History of Early Christian Doctrine*, Vol. 1 (London: Darton, Longman and Todd, 1964).

Davies, W. D., *The Setting of the Sermon on the Mount* (Cambridge: Cambridge University Press, 1966).

——, *The Sermon on the Mount* (Cambridge: Cambridge University Press, 1969).

——, "The Relevance of the Moral Teaching of the Early Church", in, E. Earle Ellis and Max Wilcox (eds.), *Neotestamentica et Semitica* (Edinburgh: Clark, 1969), 30-49.

——, and D. Daube (eds.), *The Background of the New Testament and its Eschatology* (Cambridge: Cambridge University Press, 1964).

Dawson, C., *The Dynamics of World History* (New York: Mentor Omega Books, 1962).

Derrett, J. Duncan M., *Law in the New Testament* (London: Darton, Longman and Todd, 1970).

——, "The Parable of the Prodigal Son: Patristic Allegories and Jewish Midrashim", *Studia Patristica*, 10, 1 (1970), 219-224.

——, *Jesus's Audience* (London: Darton, Longman and Todd, 1973).

——, *The Making of Mark*, 2 vols. (Shipston-on-Stour, Warwickshire: Drinkwater, 1985).

——, "The Upper Room and the Dish", *Heythrop Journal*, 26, 4 (1985), 373-382.

——, "A Camel through the Eye of a Needle", *New Testament Studies*, 32, 3 (1986), 465-470.

——, "Birds of the Air and Lilies of the Field", *Downside Review*, 360 (1987), 181-192.

Dibelius, M., *A Commentary on the Epistle of James* (11th ed., revised by Heinrich Greeven; Philadelphia: Fortress, 1976).

Dodd, C. H., *The Parables of the Kingdom* (London: Collins, 1971).

Dudden, F. Homes, *The Life and Times of St. Ambrose*, Vol. 2 (Oxford: Clarendon Press, 1935).

Dvornik, Francis, *Early Christian and Byzantine Political Philosophy*, Vol. 2 (Washington: Dumbarton Oaks Center for Byzantine Studies, 1966).

Ehrhardt, Arnold, *The Framework of the New Testament Stories* (Manchester: Manchester University Press, 1964).

Ellis, Peter F., *The Yahwist: the Bible's First Theologian* (London: Chapman, 1969).

Fedwick, Paul J., *The Church and the Charisma of Leadership in Basil of Caesarea* (Toronto: Pontifical Institute of Mediaeval Studies, 1979).

Finley, M. I., *The Ancient Economy* (London: Chatto and Windus, 1973).

Florovsky, Georges, "Empire and Desert: Antinomies of Christian History", *Greek Orthodox Theological Review*, 3 (1957), 133-159.

Fox, Margaret Mary, *The Life and Times of St. Basil the Great as Revealed in His Works* (Washington: Catholic University of America Press, 1939).

Frend, W. H. C., *The Donatist Church* (Oxford: Clarendon Press, 1971).

Fuerst, Wesley J., *The Books of Ruth, Esther, Ecclesiastes, The Song of Songs, Lamentations* (Cambridge: Cambridge University Press, 1975).

Garrett, T. M., "St. Augustine and the Nature of Society", *The New Scholasticism*, 30 (1956), 16-36.

Gill, Athol, *Christians and the Poor* (Canberra: Zadok Centre Paper, No. 9, 1979).

Goldsmith, R. W., *Premodern Financial Systems* (Cambridge: Cambridge University Press, 1987).

Goodhart, E., "Job and the Modern World", *Judaism*, 10 (1961), 21-28.

Gordis, R., *The Book of God and Man: a Study of Job* (Chicago and London: University of Chicago Press, 1973).

Gordon, Barry, *Economic Analysis Before Adam Smith: Hesiod to Lessius* (London: Macmillan, 1975).

——, "Lending at Interest: some Jewish, Greek and Christian Approaches, 800 B.C. — A.D. 100", *History of Political Economy*, 14 (1982), 406-426.

——, "Economic Welfare and Regulation of the Economy in the Pentateuch and the Mishnah", *Humanomics*, 1 (1985), 107-120.

——, "Economic Dimensions of the Revival of Israel in the Thought of the Later Jewish Prophets", in, C. Tisdell (ed.), *Contributed Economic Essays: a Collection in Memory of Dr. M. G. Kibria* (Newcastle: Department of Economics, University of Newcastle, 1987), 363-390.

——, "Biblical and Early Judeo-Christian Thought: Genesis to Augustine", in, S. Todd Lowry (ed.), *Pre-Classical Economic Thought* (Boston: Kluwer, 1987), 43-67.

Grabowski, S. J., "The Role of Charity in the Mystical Body of Christ according to Saint Augustine", *Revue Des Etudes Augustiniennes*, 3 (1957), 29-63.

Grant, F. C., "The Economic Background of the New Testament", in W. D. Davies
    and D. Daube (eds.), *The Background of the New Testament and its Eschatology* (Cam-
    bridge: Cambridge University Press, 1964), 96-114.
Grant, Robert M., *Early Christianity and Society* (London: Collins, 1978).
Gray, John, *I and II Kings, a Commentary* (London: S.C.M., 1970).
Greer, R. A., "Hospitality in the First Five Centuries of the Church", *Monastic Studies*,
    10 (1974), 29-48.
Guthrie, Donald, *Galatians* (London: Oliphants, 1977).
Haenchen, E., *The Acts of the Apostles, a Commentary* (Oxford: Blackwell, 1971).
Hall, B., "The Problem of Retribution in the Psalms", *Scripture*, 7 (1955), 84-92.
Hatch, Edwin, *The Influence of Greek Ideas on Christianity* (New York: Harper, 1957).
Havelock, Eric A., *The Liberal Temper in Greek Politics* (London: Cape, 1957).
Heaton, E. W., *The Hebrew Kingdoms* (Oxford: Oxford University Press, 1968).
Hengel, M., *Judaism and Hellenism*, 2 vols. (London: S.C.M., 1974).
——, *Property and Riches in the Early Church* (London: S.C.M., 1974).
Hill, E., "Trinitarian Politics: or towards an Augustinian Marxism?", *Prudentia*, 5
    (1973), 91-98.
Hopkins, M. K., "Social Mobility in the Later Roman Empire: the Evidence of
    Ausonius", *The Classical Quarterly*, n.s. 11 (1961), 239-248.
——, "Elite Mobility in the Roman Empire", *Past and Present*, 32 (1965), 12-26.
Houlden, J. L., *Ethics and the New Testament* (London and Oxford: Mowbrays, 1973).
Hubbard, Joseph B., *Economic Thought in Patristic Literature* (unpublished Ph.D. thesis,
    Harvard University, 1923).
Isichei, Elizabeth A., *Political Thinking and Social Experience: some Christian Interpretations of
    the Roman Empire from Tertullian to Salvian* (Christchurch: University of Canterbury
    Publications, No. 6, 1964).
Jackson, F. J. Foakes and Kirsopp Lake, *The Acts of the Apostles*, Vol. 4 (1932; Grand
    Rapids, Michigan: Baker, 1979).
Jeremias, J. J., *The Parables of Jesus* (London: S.C.M., 1972).
Jervell, Jacob, *Luke and the People of God* (Minneapolis: Augsburg, 1979).
John Paul II, Pope, *Laborem Exercens* (Aust. ed.; Sydney: St. Paul, 1981).
Jones, A. H. M., *The Later Roman Empire, 284-602*, Vol. 2 (Oxford: Blackwell, 1964).
——, *The Roman Economy* (ed. P. A. Brunt), (Oxford: Blackwell, 1974).
Jones, Alexander, "The Gospel of Jesus Christ according to St. Matthew", in, B.
    Orchard et al., *A Catholic Commentary on Holy Scripture* (London: Nelson, 1953),
    851-904.
Judge, E. A., *The Social Pattern of Christian Groups in the First Century* (London: Tyndale
    Press, 1960).
Kaiser, Otto, *Isaiah 1-12, a Commentary* (London: S.C.M., 1977).
Karris, R. J., "Poor and Rich: the Lukan Sitz im Leben", in, C. H. Talbert (ed.),
    Perspectives on Luke-Acts (Edinburgh: Clark, 1978).
Kummel, W. G., *Introduction to the New Testament* (17th, ed.; Nashville: Abingdon, 1975).
Lacocque, Andre, *The Book of Daniel* (London: S.P.C.K., 1979).
Ladner, Gerhart B., *The Idea of Reform: its impact on Christian Thought and Action in the Age
    of the Fathers* (Cambridge, Mass.: Harvard University Press, 1959).
Laistner, M. L. W., *Christianity and Pagan Culture in the Late Roman Empire* (Ithaca: Cornell
    University Press, 1951).
Liebeschuetz, J. H. W. G., *Antioch, City and Imperial Administration in the Later Roman
    Empire* (Oxford: Clarendon Press, 1972).
Lohse, E., *Colossians and Philemon* (Philadelphia: Fortress, 1971).
Linnemann, Eta, *Parables of Jesus* (London: S.P.C.K., 1975).
McKane, William, *Proverbs, a New Approach* (London: S.C.M., 1970).
McKenzie, J. L., *The Anchor Bible: Second Isaiah* (New York: Doubleday, 1968).
MacMullen, Ramsay, "Social Mobility and the Theodosian Code", *Journal of Roman
    Studies*, 54 (1964), 49-53.
McNeile, A. H., *The Gospel According to St. Matthew* (London: Macmillan, 1961).

MacQueen, D. J., "St. Augustine's Concept of Property Ownership", *Recherches Augusti-niennes*, 8 (1972), 187-229.

Maloney, R. P., "Early Conciliar Legislation on Usury", *Recherches de Theologie Ancienne et Medievale*, 39 (1972), 145-157.

——, "The Teaching of the Fathers on Usury", *Vigiliae Christianae* 27 (1973), 241-265.

Maly, E. H., *The Epistles of Saints James, Jude, Peter* (Collegeville, Minn.: Liturgical Press, 1960).

Markus, R. A., "Two Conceptions of Political Authority: Augustine, De Civitate Dei, XIX, 14-15, and some Thirteenth-Century Interpretations", *Journal of Theological Studies*, 17 (1965), 68-100.

Marshall, I. H., *The Gospel of Luke* (Exeter: Paternoster, 1978).

——, *Luke: Historian and Theologian* (Exeter: Paternoster, 1979).

Marshall, R. T., *Studies in the Political and Socio-Religious Terminology of the De Civitate Dei* (Washington: Catholic University of America Press, 1952).

Maxwell, John Francis, *Slavery and the Catholic Church* (Chichester and London: Barry Rose Publishers, for the Anti-Slavery Society for the Protection of Human Rights, 1975).

Maynard-Reid, P. U., *Poverty and Wealth in James* (Maryknoll: Orbis, 1987).

Mays, J. L., *Micha, a Commentary* (London: S.C.M., 1976).

Momigliano, Arnaldo (ed.), *The Conflict Between Paganism and Christianity in the Fourth Century* (Oxford: Clarendon Press, 1963).

Mommsen, Theodor E., "St. Augustine and the Christian Idea of Progress", *Journal of the History of Ideas*, 12 (1951), 346-374.

Moore, R. D., "The Integrity of Job", *Catholic Biblical Quarterly*, 45 (1983), 17-31.

Musurillo, Herbert, "The Problem of Ascetical Fasting in the Greek Patristic Writers", *Traditio*, 12 (1964), 1-64.

Neufeld, E., "Socio-economic background of Yobel and Semitta", *Revista Degli Studi Orientali*, 33 (1958), 53-124.

Niebuhr, H. Richard, *Christ and Culture* (New York: Harper, 1951).

Neil, William, *The Acts of the Apostles* (London: Oliphants, 1973).

North, C. R., *The Second Isaiah* (Oxford: Clarendon Press, 1964).

Noth, M., *Leviticus, a Commentary* (London: S.C.M., 1965).

O'Flynn, J., "The Gospel of Jesus Christ according to St. Mark", in B. Orchard et al., *A Catholic Commentary on Holy Scripture* (London: Nelson, 1953), 905-934.

Ohrenstein, Roman A. and Barry Gordon, "Some Aspects of Human Capital in Talmudic Literature", *International Journal of Social Economics* 14 (1987), 185-190.

Osborne, E. F., *The Philosophy of Clement of Alexandria* (London: Cambridge University Press, 1957).

Parsons, Wilfred, "The Influence of Romans XIII On Pre-Augustinian Christian Political Thought", *Theological Studies*, 1 (1940), 337-364.

Pearce, G. J. M., "Augustine's Theory of Property", *Studia Patristica*, 6 (1962), 496-500.

Pope, M. H., *The Anchor Bible: Job* (New York: Doubleday, 1973).

Porteous, N., *Daniel, a Commentary* (London: S.C.M., 1979).

Prichard, Muriel F. Lloyd, "The Roman Contribution to Economic Growth", *Prudentia*, 2 (1970), 1-5.

Rad, G. von, *Genesis, a Commentary* (London: S.C.M., 1972).

——, *Wisdom in Israel* (London: S.C.M., 1972).

Reumann, J., "Oikonomia-Terms in Paul in Comparison with Lucan 'Heilsgeschichte' ", *New Testament Studies*, 13 (1966-67), 147-167.

——, "Jesus the Steward: an Overlooked Theme in Christology", in, F. L. Cross (ed.), *Studia Evangelica*, Vol. 5 (Berlin: Akademie-Verlag, 1968), 21-29.

Rhymer, Joseph (ed.), *The Bible in Order* (London: Darton, Longman and Todd, 1975).

Richardson, A., *The Biblical Doctrine of Work* (London: S.C.M., 1958).

Robinson, J. A. T., *Redating the New Testament* (London: S.C.M., 1976).

Rowley, H. H., *The Relevance of Apocalyptic* (London: Lutterworth, 1963).

Rozsaly, F. L., "Hellenic Elements in the Dialogues of Augustine", *Classical Bulletin*, 32 (1956), 29-31.

Russell, D. S., *The Method and Message of Jewish Apocalyptic* (London: S.C.M., 1971).
Russell, K. C., "Slavery as Reality and Metaphor in the Non-Pauline New Testament Books", *Revue de l'Universite d'Ottawa*, 42 (1972), 439-469.
Schelkle, K. H., *Theology of the New Testament*, Vol. 3 (Collegeville, Minn.: Liturgical Press, 1973).
Schillebeeckx, E., *Jesus, an Experiment in Christology* (London: Collins, 1979).
Schnackenburg, R., *The Gospel According to St. John*, Vol. 1 (London: Burns and Oates, 1968).
——, *The Moral Teaching of the New Testament* (London: Burns and Oates, 1975).
Schweizer, E., *The Good News According to Matthew* (London: S.P.C.K., 1978).
Scott, R. B. Y., *The Way of Wisdom in the Old Testament* (New York: Macmillan, 1971).
Setton, Kenneth M., *Christian Attitudes Towards the Emperor in the Fourth Century* (New York: Columbia University Press, 1941).
Shewring, Walter, *Rich and Poor in Christian Tradition* (London: Burns Oates and Washbourne, 1948).
Silver, Morris, *Prophets and Markets: the Political Economy of Ancient Israel* (Boston: Kluwer-Nijhoff, 1983).
Sloyan, G. S., *The Gospel of Saint Mark* (Collegeville, Minn.: Liturgical Press, 1960).
Snaith, N., "The Prosperity of the Wicked", *Religion in Life*, 20 (1951), 519-529.
Soss, N. M., "Old Testament Law and Economic Society", *Journal of the History of Ideas*, 34 (1973), 323-344.
Stanley, D. M., "The Theme of the Servant of Yahweh in Primitive Christian Soteriology and its Transposition by St. Paul", *Catholic Biblical Quarterly*, 16 (1954), 385-425.
——, *The Gospel of St. Matthew* (Collegeville, Minn.: Liturgical Press, 1963).
Stevens, Courtenay E., "Agriculture and Rural Life in the Later Roman Empire", in, M. M. Postan (ed.), *The Cambridge Economic History of Europe*, Vol. 1 (Cambridge: Cambridge University Press, 1966), 92-124.
Stuhlmueller, Carrol, *The Gospel of Saint Luke* (Collegeville, Minn.: Liturgical Press, 1964).
Swift, Louis J., "Iustitia and Ius Privatum: Ambrose on Private Property", *American Journal of Philology*, 100 (1979), 176-187.
Tanner, R. G., "Jesus and the Fatherhood of God", *Colloquium*, 3 (1968), 201-210.
Torrey, Charles C., *Ezra Studies* (New York: Ktav, 1970).
Trimiadis, E., "Christian Love for Strangers according to the Early Fathers", *Diakonia*, 9 (1974), 234-250.
Vermes, G., *Jesus the Jew* (London: Collins, 1973).
Viner, Jacob, "The Economic Doctrines of the Christian Fathers", *History of Political Economy*, 10 (1978), 9-45.
Waldow, H. Eberhard von, "Social Responsibility and Social Structure in Early Israel", *Catholic BIblical Quarterly*, 32 (1970), 182-204.
Wansbrough, H., "St. Luke and Christian Ideals in an Affluent Society", *New Blackfriars*, 49 (1968), 582-587.
Weinfeld, M., *Deuteronomy and the Deuteronomic School* (Oxford: Clarendon Press, 1972).
Westermann, C., *Creation* (London: S.P.C.K., 1974).
——, *Isaiah 40-66: a Commentary* (London: S.C.M., 1976).
Wilken, Robert L., *The Christians as the Romans Saw Them* (New Haven: Yale University Press, 1984).
Wilkes, M. J., "The Problem of Private Ownership in Patristic Thought and an Augustinian Solution of the Fourteenth Century", *Studia Patristica*, 6 (1962), 533-542.
Williams, J. G., "What Does It Profit a Man?: the Wisdom of Koheleth", *Judaism*, 22 (1971), 179-193.
Wolff, H. W., *Joel and Amos, a Commentary* (Philadelphia: Fortress, 1977).
Wright, G. Ernest, *The Biblical Doctrine of Man in Society* (London: S.C.M., 1954).

NAME INDEX

Aaron 9
Abel 4
Abraham 5-6, 9-10, 12, 14-15, 23, 26-7, 46
Adah 4
Adam 2-6, 16, 23
Aeschylus 129
Ahlstrom, G. W. 39, 133
Albright, W. F. 9, 28, 133
Alexander the Great 40
Alfoldy, Geza 90, 97, 133
Allen, Leslie 38, 133
Amalec 115
Ambrose of Milan, Saint X, 112-20, 122, 127
Amorrhaeus 115
Amos 11
Anderson, G. W. 40, 133
Andrew the Apostle, Saint 50
Anna 62, 69
Anthony, Saint 98
Antiochus IV 40-1
Aquila 51
Arbesmann, Rudolph 97, 125-7, 133
Aristotle 34, 99-100
Armstrong, A. H. 112, 120, 133
Attwater, Donald 107-8, 133
Augustine of Hippo, Saint X, 81, 99, 106, 120-32
Azkoul, Michael 91, 133

Baker, Aelred 45, 97, 133
Barker, E. 56, 133
Barnabas 69, 78, 84
Barnes, Timothy D. 97-9, 133
Barr, R. B. 121, 133
Barrett, C. K. 44, 49, 133
Barrosse, T. 133
Barth, Markus 47, 52, 133
Basil the Great, Saint X, 81, 99, 101-9, 116
Beare, F. W. 52, 133
Bell, H. Idris 84, 134
Berry, Christopher 130, 134
Best, Ernest 52, 134
Betz, Hans Deiter 113, 134
Bezalel 15
Biard, Pierre 71, 134
Bildad 28
Boak, Arthur E. R. 89, 93-4, 96, 134
Boaz 30-1

Booth, E. 127, 134
Borne, Etienne 35, 134
Bouyer, Louis 101, 134
Breuggemann, Walter 6, 10, 134
Bright, John 12, 22, 134
Brown, Peter 99, 104, 134
Brown, Raymond E. 44-5, 66, 74, 134
Bullough, S. 81
Burt, D. X. 122, 134

Cain 4, 123
Campbell, Edward F. 30-1, 134
Campenhausen, Hans von 91, 134
Carlson, Charles P. 126, 134
Chadwick, Henry 85, 113-4
Childs, Brevard 16, 134
Chrysostom, Saint John X, 89, 101-3, 105-11, 113-4
Cicero 112, 114-5, 119-20, 122, 124
Clarke, Thomas E. 126, 134
Clement of Alexandria IX, 77, 82, 84-7, 114-5
Clement of Rome 84
Cochrane, Charles Norris 91-3, 131, 134
Columella 94
Constantelos, Demetrios 86, 102, 106-7, 134
Constantine, Emperor X, 77, 89-91
Conzelmann, H. 79, 134
Cranz, F. Edward 90, 121-2, 129-30, 134
Creed, J. M. 73, 134
Crispus 51
Cross, F. L. 54, 137
Cullman, Oscar 79, 81-2, 134
Cyprian of Carthage 82

Dahood, M. J. 35
Danielou, Jean 81, 134
Daube, David 79, 135-6
David, King 31, 33, 36
Davies, William D. 43, 46, 50, 56, 72, 74-5, 79, 134-6
Dawson, Christopher 84, 135
Derrett, J. Duncan M. 46, 48-9, 52, 56-8, 73, 80, 110, 135
Dibelius, Martin 59-61, 135
Diocletian, Emperor 93, 95, 98
Dodd, C. H. 56, 135
Dudden, F. Homes 112-3, 115, 117-9, 135

SUBJECT INDEX